A Practical Guide to
Decorative Paint Techniques

MASTER STROKES

JENNIFER BENNELL

First published in 1988 by
Random House Australia Pty Ltd
20 Alfred Street, Milsons Point NSW 2061

First published in the United States in 1991 by:
Rockport Publishers, Inc.
5 Smith Street
P.O. Box 396
Rockport, Massachusetts 01966
Tel: (508) 546-9590
Fax: (508) 546-7141

Reprinted 1991, 1993

For distribution by North Light Books, an imprint of
F&W Publications
1507 Dana Avenue
Cincinnati, Ohio 45207
Tel: (513) 531-2222
Toll-Free: 1-800-289-0963
Fax: (513) 531-4744

ISBN 0-935603-88-3

Designed by Jane Tenney
Printed in Singapore
Production by Vantage Graphics, Sydney

A Practical Guide to Decorative Paint Techniques

MASTER STROKES

JENNIFER BENNELL

Photography: Andrew Payne

Rockport Publishers — Rockport, Massachusetts
Distributed by North Light Books — Cincinnati, Ohio

Dedication

To Neil and Chlöe who bore the production of this
book with much stoicism.

Acknowledgement

I wish to thank Hazel Tate and Kevin Tenney for
contributing the Stencilling chapter. My heartfelt
thanks go to John Quirk without whose help I would
not have been able to complete this book, and I wish to
thank Judith Hardenbrook and Phyllis Statham for
their devoted help and support. Credit is also due
to photographer Andrew Payne
and stylist Robin Duffecy.

CONTENTS

1. Before. An array of untouched
pieces bought from
supermarkets and chain stores.
Household chairs, vases, jugs,
frames, candlesticks — virtually
any item in the house — can be
included in your selection.
2. After. The pieces are
transformed into a distinctive
selection of decorative and
useful objects employing all of
the simple restoration finishes
described in this book.

INTRODUCTION

BY WRITING THIS BOOK I hope to
throw open the door to this most
exciting world of painted finishes.
Often, I have heard people remark that
without artistic ability, one cannot learn,
let alone practise the art of restoration
using decorative painted finishes. I cannot
stress strongly enough the fallacy of this
commonly held belief. While obviously
someone with natural artistic ability will
master the finishes quickly, any person
willing to learn can create their own
lustrous, exotic pieces. Essentially,
painted finishes are the result of learned
techniques. They are not artistically
inspired masterpieces. The only
prerequisites necessary are enthusiasm,
attention to detail and plenty of time.

I have included a full range of finishes,
each of which can be developed using
easy-to-follow steps. Every finish

described in this book, with the exception
of the examples of *trompe l'oeil*, can be
developed systematically and quickly.
Whether or not you are gifted with brush
and pen, *Master Strokes* will enable you to
perform a myriad of finishes to restore
small decorative objects, furniture,
floors and walls.

For many years I have conducted
classes in painted finishes at my school in
Sydney. *Master Strokes* is an extension of
these classes, with step-by-step
instructions and explanation of the basic
paint preparation exercises which lead to
a choice of exciting and unusual antiquing
finishes including stippling, dragging,
chamois, sponging, distressing, spatter and
ageing with wax and pigment.

Stencilling, the popular technique
which can add a rustic, naive look to a
basic finish has been introduced and

explained by the specialist Hazel Tate. The section on bronze powder stencilling by Kevin Tenney recreates the simple though exotic coloured powder finishes which flourished during the nineteenth century. In a separate chapter the secrets of gilding are revealed, together with recipes for changing the often too-brilliant leaf to resemble pewter, aged silver and bronze.

A Western version of the Japanese lacquering process is also included. In compiling this chapter I have dared to presume that I have dealt with this delicate technique well enough to avert the wrath of Japan's famous *urushi* masters being called down upon me! You will learn how to varnish correctly and how to utilise varnish to add a smooth, tactile quality which improves the lustre of the finish. Colour mixing is presented not as an esoteric, technical treatise, but as a simple, straightforward activity. With my recipes you can achieve true colour reproduction using whatever paints you have available.

Inside almost every house there are decorative objects, furniture and wall surfaces waiting to be restored. Contrary to popular myth, paint finishes are suited to articles made from just about any material including wood, glass, ceramic, highly glazed pottery, plastic and leather. Many of the most successful painted items are bought straight off the supermarket or department store shelf. A plastic jug and matching ice bucket bought from a well-known department store can be transformed quickly and easily with a red crackle finish and gold-leaf edge. (See page 125.) Small plastic trays purchased from a chain store and given a new finish make a stylish addition to dressing tables and coffee tables, or to hold salt and pepper on the dining table. Tin and plastic wastepaper baskets take painted finishes well and can be lined inside with marble paper which is then protected by a coat of varnish. Virtually any of the objects in use from day to day can be completely overhauled, rejuvenated and recreated using new paint finishes. Glass vases, tin canisters, filing boxes and old table mats are just a few examples.

One of the most important considerations when choosing a piece of furniture or a decorative object to restore is firstly to isolate and define its good design qualities. A clumsy, ill-conceived chair with thick, ungainly legs will never be enhanced by a new decorative finish. Remember that painted finishes require a considerable investment of time and energy. It is foolish to try and transform a badly designed piece using a new paint finish that will only exaggerate its ugly appearance.

Learning about decorating and restoring using special paint finishes is an obsessive process. Even now, when I see or am shown a new technique, I still experience the same excitement I felt when I sat in my first class many years ago with the famed Gale Laurence in San Francisco. The effects which can be created using paint finishes open up a simple yet wondrous world of decorating and design opportunities for everyone.

Jennifer Bennell

1

SETTING UP
A WORKSHOP

JUST AS COOKING requires the use of special utensils in a specific area of the house, so must painted finishes be prepared and executed in their own working space. Regrettably the preparatory work cannot be carried about in a pretty basket, deposited in a chair and the piece worked on while you partake of cups of tea and genteel conversation. There are those who object to a piece of wood being heartily sanded in the drawing room. Others may become alarmed at the sight of a brush and bucket of mineral turpentine left on the bedroom floor. In this chapter I explain how to make a practical working area in whatever space you have available, even the tiniest corner of the house. Necessary tools are listed and some basic guidelines are set out for cleaning and storing your equipment.

THE IDEAL WORKSHOP IS SPACIOUS and light, with extensive shelving, cupboards and storage space. When space is at a premium an efficient area can be created simply by fitting out a large cupboard with shelves and a card table that can be folded and put aside when necessary. The cupboard may be located in a bathroom, a hallway, a bedroom or even at one end of a kitchen. If working in a kitchen the work should be kept as far away as possible from the cooking area as the fumes from the finishes are flammable and may cause an explosion or catch on fire and damage the whole area.

Ventilation is of prime importance. A constant flow of fresh air through the work place will disperse and dilute any dangerous fumes. The area that you work in should also be as clean as possible. Stray dust particles can gather on sticky wet surfaces and ruin a freshly painted piece.

Wherever you work, it is advisable to have shelves close by to store often-used equipment. Tools such as hammers and screwdrivers can be hung on an easily-constructed pegboard at the back of the shelves or on the side of the cupboard. Finally, good lighting is essential. If the work area is not blessed with good natural light, an extra light should be fitted overhead. A corrected light, simulating daylight, provides an excellent alternative to natural light.

SUPPLIES

The following list of items is essential to any paint workshop. The list should be treated as a frequently-used grocery list and diminishing stocks should be consistently replenished.

MINERAL TURPENTINE/MINERAL SPIRITS
This (highly flammable) liquid is used for thinning paint, for cleaning paint surfaces and for cleaning brushes. Do not buy artists' gum turpentine as it is toxic and more expensive than mineral turpentine. Mineral turpentine can be bought in most supermarkets and hardware shops.

METHYLATED SPIRITS/MINERAL ALCOHOL
Methylated spirits is used for mixing with bleached white shellac, for cleaning off old shellac and stain finishes and for cleaning the shellac brush.

SANDPAPER
You can never have enough of this rough, reddish coloured paper, an important material for your finishes. The various types of sandpaper include:

60 grit: This coarse paper is used on very rough wood, or on furniture which has been poorly painted with gloss enamel paint or varnish. A word of warning: it is possible to damage some surfaces with this sandpaper. Once this grit has been used, it should be followed by careful smoothing with finer sandpaper (220).

80 grit: A similar, yet finer paper than the above.

100 grit: Medium grit is used most for sanding after filling has been completed and the surface has dried. Be careful not to damage the surrounding surface when using this sandpaper. The coarseness or strength of the sandpaper will smooth the filler but it may be too harsh for the surrounding material. When filling the grain of oak wood, for example, use 100 grit sandpaper. (Fine filling is dealt with in a following chapter.)

220 grit: Once you have achieved as perfect a finish as possible, use 220 grit sandpaper to finish off.

400 wet and dry: This sandpaper is black in colour and is used for another step called 'tuffbacking' or wet-sanding, using water. Wet-sanding is one of the final processes used in the later stages of preparation for antiquing. The final basecoat of paint should be wet-sanded before the antiquing medium or decorative finish is applied. This process is also applied to the final coat of varnish.

600 wet and dry: This slightly finer grit of 600 wet and dry sandpaper requires a little more effort to obtain the desired result.

1200 wet and dry: A very fine sandpaper, used for the final wet-sanding of very refined painted and varnished surfaces.

STEEL WOOL
Steel wool is frequently used to obtain a good sanded surface, however, it should be used with care. It should not be used on pale colours as it can discolour the paint. Raised areas that cannot be abraded with sandpaper should be sanded with steel wool. In Australia steel wool is available in two strengths, whereas in the UK and the USA hardware stores stock four strengths. The finer the wool, the better.

Hence if you live in Australia, buy a hank of steel wool from a supermarket and to gain a softer texture rub two pieces together for a few minutes.

SCOURING PADS

In some instances it is impossible to use steel wool on paint. If, for example, shellac has been applied over a pastel colour, or pastel paint has been applied to a carved surface, scouring pads should be used. The best pads to use are those manufactured specially for cleaning operating theatres. These can be bought from cleaning suppliers and paint supply shops. Do not use kitchen scourers as they may leave coloured stripes on your finish.

FILLERS

There is a huge variety of different fillers available. Powdered fillers or ready-mixed fine fillers are eminently suitable.

GLUE

Water-based glue should always be on hand for small repair jobs. Antique pieces should be repaired with water-based glue only. Modern two-pack glues should not be used on antiques but they can be used for repairing other pieces.

MASKING TAPE

It is wise to buy the best quality masking tape. Cheap masking tape will leave a residue of glue behind and even pull off your finish. You should stock up on a range of tape widths from 5 cm through to 3 mm; available at hardware stores and graphic artists' suppliers. If masking tape is to be kept for some months, it should be stored in a cool place in an airtight jar or a tightly sealed plastic bag to prevent the glue from drying out.

SHELLAC

Shellac, known as French Polish in Australia, is used as a sealing agent and as an isolator. When isolating, it is laid over a painted surface to provide a buffer between that surface and the antiquing glaze which is to be applied over it. Because of this isolating coat, the antiquing glaze can be subsequently removed, if necessary, without causing damage to the paint surface underneath.

Shellac is derived from the excreta of insects which proliferate on trees in India, Thailand and Burma. The excreta is scraped from the trees,

melted, purified, dried and chipped into small flakes. The name comes from *lac,* an Indian word for the quantity of one hundred thousand. Deep orange coloured shellac is commonly sold in hardware stores, and bleached white shellac, often sold as French Polish, is used in painted finishes.

Shellac is thinned with methylated spirits. It is worth noting that the composition of shellac/methylated spirits differs from country to country. In America, shellac is made up with a low proportion of methylated spirits, rendering it far more difficult to use than the Australian variety.

Always check the date on the shellac bottle as the substance has a limited shelf life of 12-18 months (Australia). If you are uncertain as to how old the shellac is, remove a little from the bottle and mix it with some methylated spirits. If it discolours discard it as it will remain sticky and will not dry.

BLEED SEALER

Late Victorian and Edwardian wood stains and varnishes were often constituted from aniline dyes, particularly to create mahogany and cherry stains. Aniline dyes are guaranteed to bleed through any coat of paint other than an aluminium based paint. Therefore when restoring furniture it is important to establish whether the piece has been stained with this substance. Aluminium Flake Paint should be used to give a cover over an aniline stain before a base coat of flat enamel is applied.

WAX

A special wax made of *carnauba* is easily absorbed into wood or paint. Carnauba, extracted from the leaf of a palm tree grown in Brazil, does not leave any residue, protects and gives a good sheen.

SCUMBLING MEDIUM/GLAZE COAT

In America this substance is generally referred to as glaze coat. An essential component of an antiquing glaze, scumbling medium gives the paint body, extends the drying time slightly and allows finishes to be applied to a vertical surface without the risk of sagging or dripping. The imprint of the brush or tool being used on a wall or a piece of furniture is left without the paint closing up and drying into an opaque surface. Scumbling medium allows the paler background colour to shine through to the surface when required and is necessary for all glazes.

TACK CLOTH
This piece of cheesecloth impregnated with linseed oil is used to pick up the final specks of dust after cleaning off any sanding residue. It is absolutely essential to follow three steps when sanding: sand, wipe with a soft cotton cloth — and then wipe with the tack cloth. The tack cloth must be stored in a screw-top jar to stop it drying out.

BRUSH CLEANER
Careful cleaning ensures the long life of brushes. A soapy disinfectant or proprietary brand brush cleaner used in conjunction with hot water gives the best results on most brushes used for paint finishes.

PAINT
It is essential to use oil-based flat enamel paints to create fine, smooth finishes. Water-based paint gives a coarse finish and does not sand well. It is impossible to obtain a fine finish with water-based paint. Oil-based flat enamel paint will go a surprisingly long way. You only need store about one litre of white paint and 250 mls of black paint.

JAPAN PAINT
This style of paint came into use when the Europeans began to copy Japanese and Chinese lacquer techniques in the 17th and 18th centuries. It was the paint used by coach painters during that period. The Venetians first simulated these finishes and the technique was later referred to in Britain as 'japanning', hence the name for the paint. Flat and opaque, the paint is also very intense in colour.

ASPHALTUM
Used as an overglaze and in tortoiseshell finishes, asphaltum can be bought at specialty shops.

VARNISH
There are two principal types of suitable varnish. Marine varnish offers a particularly tough finish, but its amber colour can discolour a pale finish. Otherwise, normal household varnish — in flat, satin and gloss — is commonly used. This also discolours, being slightly yellow.

SURGICAL GLOVES
Use tight-fitting surgical gloves, available from your chemist or drug store. (Ill-fitting household gloves tend to be unwieldy when performing fine finishes.)

UPHOLSTERY/COTTON WADDING
Cotton wadding is used when isolating, and also instead of sponges in some antiquing glazes. Ordinary cotton wool must not be used as it becomes a tight, rock-like ball when placed in shellac.

ANILINE DYES
Aniline dyes, of which you were warned in the section on bleed sealer above, carefully used in small quantities, can give a realistic aged effect. Warm, reddish-brown tones, and cool, greenish-brown tones are the most commonly used. The dyes come in powder form and are made up with shellac as the fixing element and methylated spirits as the thinner.

Warning: These dyes are toxic and must not be inhaled or come into contact with the skin.

OTHER SUPPLIES
Other useful materials to have on hand are pure cotton cloths (T-shirt material is ideal), chopsticks (for stirring paint), tins and screw-top jars, newspapers, butchers' paper and rubber bands.

ESSENTIAL TOOLS

GOOD EQUIPMENT is of prime importance if you intend to obtain perfect results. The following list covers the bare minimum of tools required.

SHELLAC BRUSH
This brush is a 3.8 cm cutter made of black bristle and used by house-painters for cutting in around windowsills and architraves etc. It should be reserved exclusively for sealing with shellac.

OXHAIR BRUSH
Used for applying paint, this is a very fine brush (2.5 cm) which does not leave hairmarks. In Australia these brushes are sold as imitation sable although they are generally made of oxhair. Soft, fine nylon brushes can also be used as an alternative.

NO. 6 BRIGHT
The general workhorse brush, is used for painting shellac on tricky carved areas, in corners and on edges. It is also used in paint for striping and for painting difficult areas.

FITCH

This 2.5 cm brush is used specifically for the dragging process.

BRISTLE STIPPLE BRUSH

Not to be confused with a stencil brush which looks much the same, but has a very flat, cut-off head, the bristle stipple brush is used to apply many antiquing glazes. It is worth buying several different sizes. (In the USA it is called a pounce brush.)

NO. 003 SABLE

This brush is used for striping and imposing designs.

NO. 000 SABLE

Used for application of fine designs.

BRISTLE BRUSHES (2.5 cm)

Buy a dozen of these cheaply from the supermarket to make into spatter brushes.

FOAM PAD BRUSHES (2.5 cm)

Wonderful for applying varnish to large areas. The varnish is applied with a foam brush then laid off (stroked out) with an oxhair brush. Foam pad brushes are also useful for applying glazes quickly to large areas. Though normally considered disposable, they can be re-used many times if cleaned in turpentine and wrapped in a plastic air-tight wrap. Do not wash in soap and water as they will fall apart.

CHAMOIS

This tool is used to create the effect of marble, to give the appearance of crushed velvet or to make large, stone-like eruptions in marble. Pure chamois gives a better effect than the synthetic version. If chamois is washed out in turpentine and then in soapy disinfectant, it will last through many applications of paint.

13

SPONGE

Sponges give soft, cloud-like effects and stone and marble effects. Once again, you must use real sea sponges. Synthetic sponges create too harsh an outline. Wash sponges in mineral turpentine and soapy disinfectant and rinse well. Sponges will last even longer than chamois if cared for properly.

GRAINING COMB

This comb creates a variety of designs and is used to simulate the appearance of wood grain. On large areas such as floors a graining comb achieves an interesting textured look quickly and effortlessly.

HEART-OF-WOOD GRAINING TOOL

Used to create the appearance of the heart of wood grain, this tool is perfect for panelling and doors.

SOFTENER

A substitute brush for the extremely expensive badger blender, the softener, as its name suggests, softens the harsher edges of a tool such as the heart-of-wood graining tool above. It can also be used to soften and blend outlines in marble.

CLEANING YOUR TOOLS

CLEANING SHOULD BECOME an automatic activity at the end of each session spent painting. It is most important that all brushes are carefully rinsed after use. Have ready two or three tins full of mineral turpentine. Once you are finished, you can sit the brushes in turpentine for some hours.

In my studio I have three large (three-litre) cans. In each I have suspended wire strainers. The handles have been cut from the strainers and pieces of wire inserted in the sides and strung over the top of the tin. The strainers and brushes are suspended in the mineral turpentine so that they do not sit in sludge at the bottom of the can. This way the turpentine can be used for many weeks and when it needs changing it can easily be emptied off. Sludge from the bottom of the can should be scraped off onto paper, wrapped up and discarded.

Warning: Do not scrape onto newspaper as the combination is flammable.

Foam pad brushes are used to apply varnish or glazes to large areas.

The heart-of-wood graining tool and the triangular graining comb are used to create a variety of designs.

A softener, used for softening the edges left by tools in glazes.

If a brush or brushes harden, dip them into a saucepan containing boiling water, detergent and ammonia. (Be careful of the fumes.) Alternatively, immerse the brush in paint stripper for a short time.

To clean a brush which has been used in oil-based paint or varnish, dip in two or three baths of mineral turpentine (varnish brushes should be washed in mineral turpentine reserved for that purpose only). Place soapy disinfectant in a separate container and wash brush. Finally, rinse in very hot water and pull through a clean piece of towelling to remove as much water as possible. Re-shape the brush and pull across a cake of pure soap to replace the manufacturer's size. Then hang upside down to dry. (This prevents water rotting the ferrule.) The next day, flick the brush to make sure the bristles are soft and that there is no stiffness remaining. If the brush is still stiff repeat the washing procedure. Brushes should be stored standing on their handles in an upright container. When carrying brushes from one place to another they should be carefully packed so that they do not roll around and get damaged.

Shellac is quite difficult to remove from brushes. Shellac brushes should be cleaned in the same way as the paint brushes. This is done by first using methylated spirits instead of mineral turpentine — and secondly continuing with the soapy detergent wash as described above.

Foam pads can be washed in mineral turpentine several times until they come clean. Soap and water will remove the glue. They should then be wrapped in cling wrap to prevent the air drying them out. If they start to come apart use a few drops of an epoxy glue to hold them together.

To clean graining tools, use an old toothbrush and mineral turpentine and then wash in the soapy detergent cleaner and hot water. The heart-of-wood tool

A unique textural pattern transforms a red chain store table on which a black glaze has been painted. The heart-of-wood and the graining comb has been applied.

and the graining comb are cleaned in this way, although if left to soak for any length of time in mineral turpentine they may turn into a rubbery mess at the bottom of the strainer.

Sponges and chamois are rinsed first in mineral turpentine, then in the soapy detergent cleaner and hot water. They should be thoroughly rinsed. These tools will harden and become absolutely useless if any paint residue is left after washing.

Warning: Never use a brush which has been wet with water in oil-based paint. If you need to wash your brush and use it immediately, or realise it will not have enough time to dry, wash it through five baths of mineral turpentine and pull through a cloth to remove excess turpentine. It will then be suitable for use. Shellac brushes can also be washed out in five baths of methylated spirits.

2

PREPARATION FOR RESTORATION

A typical example of an elegant chair beyond its prime and about to receive a new suit of clothes. As part of the preparatory process, the chair must be stripped using paint stripper and caustic soda.

A PERFECTLY PREPARED ITEM of furniture or a small decorative object is no less than a delight to handle — as well as being a pleasure to look at. The essence of the finishes presented in these chapters lies in their preparation. It is absolutely pointless spending many hours working on mastering the finishes if you omit any of the steps in the process, particularly in the early stages of preparation. The desire to skip just one of the sandings of one coat of paint is often present but it must be ignored at all costs. Flaws from careless or reduced sanding will glare through the final finish abysmally, as will brush strokes and imperfect applications of paint and varnish. It is essential to follow this chapter for complete instruction in sanding, filling, sealing and the various treatments required for restoring surfaces which have already been French-polished, varnished or painted.

CAREFUL PREPARATION is indeed the essence of a fine painted finish. A piece which has been insufficiently prepared will betray surface imperfections such as a rough grain or unfilled holes with the result that the finish may lose the look of lustrous, aged splendour which can only be achieved through a meticulous step-by-step process.

STRIPPING

Firstly, determine whether it is necessary to strip the piece back to its original state. A painted, varnished or French-polished object may only require superficial sanding back to a smooth, almost perfect state before the initial coat of paint is applied. If the piece has been carelessly painted with high gloss enamel paint or varnish with drips and sags visible in the finished coat, it will have to be stripped back thoroughly. There are several methods of stripping, each of which is employed for a specific purpose. Where possible, the stripping procedure should be carried out outdoors, or if inside, on a concrete floor in a well ventilated room. The fumes given off by the stripper are dangerous and may injure if inhaled.

STRIPPING WITH CAUSTIC SODA
This is a very harsh method which has proven particularly successful on pieces already painted in resistant finishes such as gloss enamel.

Materials:

+ *Metal scrapers*
+ *Steel wool*
+ *Wet and dry sandpaper*
+ *Razor blades*
+ *Plumbers' gloves (or household gloves)*
+ *Vinegar for neutralising*
+ *Cotton cloths*
+ *Running water*

Method: Put on gloves and place one tablespoon of caustic soda and one litre of boiling water in a plastic bucket, taking care to stay clear of the fumes. Wait until it stops bubbling, load the caustic soda onto a cloth and start wiping the piece. If the caustic soda comes into contact with the skin, quickly sluice running water over it and apply vinegar. As the caustic soda tends to run down the gloves, it is useful to rub vaseline onto your arm before starting. This will stop the caustic soda from burning.

While wiping the piece with caustic soda loaded onto a cloth, use the scraper, steel wool and/or razor blade to start removing the paint. Continually wash down the piece with running water to neutralise the caustic soda. Once the stripping is completed and the caustic soda washed away with water, wipe with vinegar to neutralise the effects of the caustic soda.

PROPRIETARY BRANDS OF PAINT STRIPPER
Proprietary paint strippers provide an excellent means to strip back furniture. Once again the place of work must be well ventilated in order to allow the fumes to escape. The stripper should be applied with an old brush (do not use a good brush as it will be ruined). If the paint or varnish proves difficult to move, leave the piece in a warm sunny place and watch the paint or varnish start blistering. Wash it off with water and rub over with vinegar.

STRIPPER AND CAUSTIC SODA
On painted surfaces which are particularly difficult to remove, use stripper first, then wash down the piece with caustic soda. Although this is a harsh way of handling the wood, it works. The piece must be carefully washed off with water and rubbed over with plenty of vinegar to neutralise.

COMMERCIAL STRIPPING
An alternative to this do-it-yourself stripping process is commercial stripping. The pieces are taken to a commercial stripping shop where they are immersed in a bath of caustic soda. This is a quick and effortless way to have furniture stripped back but it does have its pitfalls. Back street commercial stripping operators should be avoided. If the piece is left in caustic soda for too long and the soda is not carefully neutralised a white residue will start to exude from the wood sometime later.

ANILINE STAIN
Occasionally a piece will have been finished in a combination of either varnish and aniline dye, or French polish (shellac) and aniline dye. These dyes, used in Victorian and Edwardian times before the invention of modern stains, can wreak disastrous havoc beneath a paint finish. To ascertain whether the finish is varnish or French polish, soak a piece of

used steel wool in methylated spirits and rub over the finish. French polish will start to come away almost immediately, while varnish will not be moved by methylated spirits. (Shellac-based finishes will strip off easily with methylated spirits. Old varnish is removed with caustic soda or stripper). It is sometimes difficult to determine whether the stain is aniline dye. If the colour seems to remain in patches in the wood, treat it as aniline dye.

It is absolutely imperative to seal in the aniline dye stain. For example, if patches of a cherry stain remain in a wooden table they will bleed through five white base coats as a bright pink. (In this case, the only possible solution is to antique the table in pink.) Aniline stains should always be sealed in with aluminium-based paint. After all filling, sanding and (shellac) sealing is completed, apply one coat of this paint and proceed in the normal fashion, applying the base coats of paint. The aluminium sealer is also excellent for sealing intense wall colours and ink marks. Use one coat and proceed in the normal fashion.

SANDING

Sanding is crucial to the preparation of a piece for a painted finish. In order to prepare the piece, you must be aware of the different types of paper and their ability to give a smooth surface ready for painting.

Firstly, remove all hardware, handles, escutcheons etc. from the piece. Examine it to see whether there are any nail heads that need to be sunk or holes and pits that should be filled. Now the whole piece must be sanded. The work area must be covered with newspaper so that all sanding residue can be discarded following each sanding session. The grit of the sandpaper you use will be determined by the condition of the wood or material on which you are working. Sandpaper which is too coarse can cause a great deal of damage, leaving deep scratch marks. Take a whole sheet of sandpaper, fold it and cut into sixteen pieces measuring approximately 7 x 7.5 cm. A piece of sandpaper this size is the most economical and easy to use. Large pieces of sandpaper are difficult to control.

Hold the sandpaper between the thumb and first three fingers. Apply it to the wood, moving back and

Hold the sandpaper between the thumb and three fingers and sand in short, straight strokes. Wipe the surface with a cotton cloth and again with a tack cloth.

forth in short straight strokes following the grain. When you have completed one length of sanding return to where you commenced at a point beside the previous sanding. Make sure you overlap the already sanded area and leave no section unsanded. Keep a soft cloth at hand to wipe off your work. Watch the wood, and feel it with your fingertips to establish that you are achieving the required finish. As soon as the sandpaper becomes clogged with dust discard it.

The sanding activity must always follow the grain of the timber unless the piece on which you are working does not have a grain (e.g. craftwood or masonite), in which case you may sand along the longest plane. This way any imperfections will not be so obvious. Remember that all marks show up through paint and are magnified under varnish.

When the initial sanding is completed, wipe with a soft cotton cloth. Discard the paper and dust from the sanding and wipe all over with the tack cloth. Remember that once the tack cloth is taken out of its protective bag, it should be stored in a small screw-top jar to stop it drying out.

A dilapidated bamboo sofa received a new coat of paint using the "cheat's" method. All it required was a trip to a commercial stripper where the previous paint was removed. It was then prepared and sprayed professionally: quick, easy and no mess.

FILLING

If the piece has large cracks, use a ready-mixed filler. A palette knife is used to fill smaller holes such as those left by sunken nails. Spoon the filler into any cracks or crevices in the piece, leaving a slight mound over each hole to allow for shrinkage. Larger cracks require more filler which may need to be applied in successive portions over a few days. This will ensure that the filler is dry and all shrinkage has occurred. Do not forget that the final painted finish will be inspected at close range and that even the slightest flaw in the application of filler may show up in the final finish.

When the filling is absolutely dry, sand back with either 80, 100 or 220 grit sandpaper, depending on the size of the crack to be filled and the condition of the wood surrounding the crack. If the wood is very rough and the filling is large, use 80 and 100. If the crack is large but surrounded by very fine wood use 100 sandpaper on the filling only.

FINE FILLING

Some types of wood have highly defined grains. For example, oak will not take a paint finish properly unless the grain is filled (except when it is painted with a wash intended to allow the grain to come through — in this instance it looks wonderful).

Successful fine filling can be achieved by diluting the filler with mineral turpentine and painting onto the open grain with a stiff brush. Sometimes it is necessary to give the piece two or three painstaking coats of this filler to achieve the desired result. Each application must be sanded carefully once it is thoroughly dry.

A commercial sanding sealer may be painted on, usually requiring two or three coats. Another useful product for this operation is wood grain filler. This filler achieves good results when rubbed into the grain with a piece of hessian (called burlap in the USA) or cloth.

The grain has successfully been filled if, having been sealed with shellac and painted with one coat of paint, no grain is apparent. If the grain shows through, wipe off the paint, or leave to dry (twenty-four hours) and brush on another coat of filler. Careful sanding of the fine filler is essential before proceeding to the next step.

SHELLAC SEALING

Every filling must be sealed with shellac. This prevents patched areas showing up through the paint finish. (This also applies to wall finishes — see Chapter 12: Wall Glazes). If the entire piece is raw, seal the complete area, including the filled pieces. Wood which has been stripped is treated as raw and sealed with shellac. If the piece has already been painted or varnished and is in good enough condition

1. Open-grained wood is filled, left, with thinned filler and with fine grain filler, right. 2. Rubbing in fine grain filler with a piece of cotton folded over thumb and index finger.

SHELLAC SEALING

1. Seal raw wood with bleached white shellac, using a 38mm cutter. Dip the cutter into the shellac about 1 cm. Remember not to overload the cutter. 2. Using the No. 6 bright, seal the outside edges, taking care not to let any drips remain. A lightly loaded brush is critical here. 3. Using 220 sandpaper, sand the shellacked wood to a silken smooth finish. Wipe with a soft cotton cloth and then with a tack cloth.

for the base coats to be painted over the original finish (having been well sanded and cleaned first) then only the filled areas need be sealed. It is possible to use orange shellac for this sealing operation. (Orange shellac is a cheaper version of bleached white shellac which may be bought in flake-form and made up at home. It should not be used in any other painted finishes.)

Method: Pour a small amount of bleached white shellac into a small tin so that it is simple to load onto the brush. Take a cutter and dip it into the shellac to about half or one centimetre up the bristles of the brush. Be careful not to overload the brush. Start by stroking on the shellac, following the grain of the wood. You will see that it is very quickly absorbed into the wood. Re-load the brush very lightly and continue in quick, straight strokes. Do not allow drips of shellac to roll over the edges.

Shellac has many strange properties, not least of which is that although it is a quick-drying material (usually about twenty minutes) it does not necessarily dry on an area where there is a heavy inundation. In this case it can be wiped off with methylated spirits. Slight irregularities in the cover of the shellac do not matter; the important consideration is that the wood is sealed all over.

Excess drips or heavy accumulations of shellac can also be wiped off with cotton dipped in methyl-ated spirits. When sealing a carved piece do not allow the shellac to drip and puddle in the carving. Use the No. 6 bright brush to paint over the shellac if the carved piece is small. For larger areas, use the cutter, loaded with extreme care so that no drops of shellac are left in the carving. It may be easier to sand these delicate areas with steel wool rather than sandpaper. However, once the area takes its first coat of paint (especially if the colour is pale), a scouring pad rather than steel wool should be used to prevent the paint from discolouring.

Cabinet makers often wet wood in order to raise the last of the grain of the wood, resulting in a lengthy drying period. Shellac performs exactly this and is dry in twenty minutes. To sand, take a piece of 220 sandpaper and carefully rub down the whole piece. The shellac may seem a little resistant to the sanding but persevere until a satin-smooth texture appears. You will find the result quite miraculous. Wipe with a clean cotton cloth and with the tack cloth. The piece is now ready to be painted.

When the sealing is finished, pour the excess shellac into a clean screw-top jar. Do not put it back into the container from which you poured it. The methylated spirits in shellac begins to evaporate as soon as the mixture is poured from the bottle. This safety measure ensures that you do not use dried out shellac in later, more important operations. Save this shellac for sealing.

PREPARING METAL

Metal pieces such as old tin trunks and trays can also take painted finishes successfully. First, strip any existing paint from the piece. It is better to start a finish on raw metal as new paint chips easily from a piece which has many layers of paint. One of the most efficient ways of doing this is to have the piece sandblasted. This operation cleans off all the marks and includes a good spray of anti-rust. The piece can then be sanded, sealed (first seal the anti-rust with a coat of shellac), sanded again and painted. Treat metal exactly as if it were wood; if the piece is not sandblasted, it must be stripped completely. If there is any sign of rust it must be cleaned off and the area then painted with a commercial rust killer. Base coats can be applied in the normal fashion.

CHECKLIST

1. All nail heads must be sunk, and holes must be filled, sanded and sealed with shellac.
2. All holes and cracks should be filled, sanded and sealed with shellac.
3. If the wood is open grained, fine fill, sand and seal with shellac.
4. If the wood is raw, seal the entire object.
5. Sand the entire object to satin-smoothness.
6. Wipe off the entire object with a cotton cloth, and then with a tack cloth.
7. If the object has been stained with aniline dye, follow all of the above and then apply one coat of aluminium flake paint.

PAINTING

The technique of painting requires just as much concentration as the stripping, filling and sanding processes. Once the specially-prepared base coats of paint are applied, the piece or object makes a giant step towards the desired finish.

Antiquing finishes are always worked from light to dark, so if in doubt about what colour to use, prepare the piece with the standard five base coats of white or off-white paint. The final mixed antiquing glaze of any colour will lie happily over this base.

Good quality flat oil-based white (or off-white)

enamel paint can be bought from any supplier. To buy this off-white shade already mixed simply consult a paint colour chart and buy the palest shade of off-white. Once thinned with mineral turpentine the paint will make up the equivalent of at least two to three times its original quantity.

Materials:

- ✦ *Oxhair brush*
- ✦ *Mineral turpentine*
- ✦ *Tack cloth*
- ✦ *Cotton cloths*
- ✦ *Small tins*

1. Using the oxhair brush, apply paint in thin, even strips. The brush must not be overloaded.

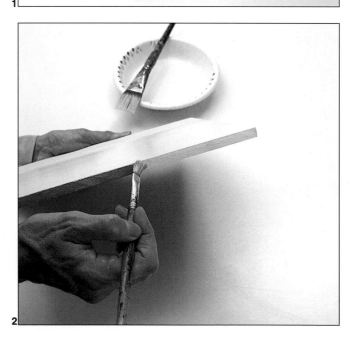

2. Use the No. 6 bright for painting the edges. Make sure no drips or overloading occur.

Method: Remove the lid from a can of paint and stir thoroughly. Take a 250 gram tin and fill three-quarters full with the paint. Add one or two tablespoons of mineral turpentine and stir well, using the wide end of double chopsticks. Take a clean, large screw-top jar and cover its top with a piece of fine hosiery. Make a well in the centre of the hosiery and secure it to the jar with a rubber band. Pour the paint slowly through the stocking. If it seems too thick to pass through the material easily, stir in a little more mineral turpentine. The strained paint should be free of any lumps and impurities.

Pour approximately two tablespoons of strained paint into a small tin. Thin with a small amount of mineral turpentine until the consistency of the paint is similar to thin cream. This runny paint helps to eliminate brush strokes on the paint surface.

The paint is applied from the tin rather than from the jar so that if an error is made when thinning, the thicker paint is still left in the jar. If the jar of paint receives too much thinner, stand it overnight or for a couple of days with the lid off until the excess mineral turpentine has evaporated.

Immediately before the paint is applied, check that the ventilation and lighting in the work area are sufficient. Dust the work area thoroughly and run the tack cloth over the piece to be painted. Load the oxhair brush into the paint about 1.5 cm. Start first on the least obvious surfaces. By the time the most exposed part of the piece is reached your consistent painting rhythm will allow the piece to be completed flawlessly. Covering only small sections at a time, lay the paint on first in one direction and then at right angles, working in thin strips about the width of the brush. As soon as each strip is covered bring the brush back over that area, smoothing the paint in straight lines. This technique, called 'laying off', must be accomplished rapidly as the paint will start to set and show up brush strokes.

Working quickly, paint and lay off until the area is covered. On small sections such as edges and carvings use the small brush, No. 6 bright. When the painting is completed, check all over for drips. Smooth any wet drips out with an index finger dipped in mineral turpentine. If the paint is setting, wait until it has dried, then take a razor blade or an X-acto knife and gently scrape away the irregularities.

The brush should be wet with paint to a point only halfway up the hairs. The painted piece should be placed on top of empty cans to dry. Pour the left-over paint into the screw-top jar. A thin layer of mineral turpentine over the top of the paint will prevent air from drying the paint out. Place two or three pieces of cling wrap immediately over the mineral turpentine and secure the screw-top.

After the piece has dried overnight or for twenty-four hours, sand it very lightly with 220 sandpaper to remove any brush strokes or irregularities — and to

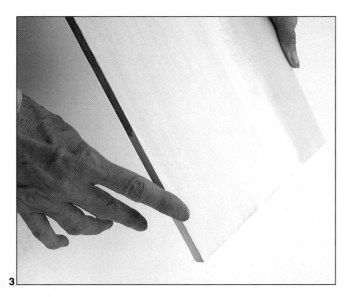

3. Now run your index finger lightly around the edges of the board to remove any build-up or overruns.

4. After the paint has dried for 24 hours sand lightly using 220 sandpaper.

create a tooth to hold the next coat of paint. Repeat the same preparatory directions as for the first coat of paint, and apply the second coat. Continue in this fashion for another three coats. A total of five coats of paint comprises the normal preparation for a piece of furniture or a small decorative object. This will give a beautiful depth of paint with its own special qualities, far superior to the effect given by one thick coat.

CHECKLIST

1. Pour a small amount of paint into a 250 gram tin and thin slightly with mineral turpentine.
2. Strain into a screw-top jar through a piece of fine hosiery.
3. Pour a small amount (62.5 grams) of strained paint into another tin. Thin to the consistency of thin cream.
4. Wipe piece to be painted with the tack cloth. Load oxhair brush carefully to 1 cm or 1.5 cm up hairs.
5. Paint on carefully, strip by strip, pulling out or laying off at the end of each strip so that the paint is smooth.
6. Leave to dry overnight or for twenty-four hours, held off the drying surface by empty tins.
7. Sand with 220 sandpaper. Wipe twice, first with a cotton cloth, then the tack cloth.
8. Stir the paint, pour a small amount into a small tin and thin with mineral turpentine.
9. Apply the second coat of paint. Allow to dry overnight or for twenty-four hours.
10. Sand with 220 sandpaper. Wipe twice, first with a cotton cloth, then the tack cloth.
11. Stir paint, thin and apply the third coat of paint. Allow to dry overnight .
12. Sand with 220 sandpaper. Wipe twice, first with a cotton cloth, then the tack cloth.
13. Stir the paint, thin if necessary and apply the fourth coat of paint. Allow to dry overnight.
14. Sand with 220 sandpaper. Wipe twice, first with a cotton cloth, then the tack cloth.
15. Stir paint. Apply the fifth coat of paint. Allow to dry overnight or for twenty-four hours. The piece is now ready to be wet-sanded.

WET-SANDING

Wet-sanding, often referred to as 'tuffbacking' creates a superb tactile texture on a piece while also adding to its visual quality. The presentation of the final finish depends very much upon this activity. Wet-sanding occurs after the application of the fifth coat of paint. It also occurs during varnishing. (See Chapter 5.)

Materials:

- *400 wet and dry sandpaper*
- *Warm water*
- *Clean cotton cloths*
- *An old towel or sheet*

Method: Before starting this process, lay an old towel or sheet on the work area and place the piece to be sanded on it. Do not work on newspaper as the print will bleed onto the paint surface. If newsprint marks the wet-sanded paint surface, remove with mineral turpentine.

Take the 400 wet and dry sandpaper, wet well and start sanding the painted surface using a circular motion. Sand in the same direction in which you painted, that is, following the grain of the wood (or, if there is no grain, follow the longer plane). The surface should be treated a small section at a time. When one length of the piece is completed, return to the adjoining unsanded area and overlap the previous wet-sanding with the new section. This way, no area should be left unsanded.

Do not let water remain too long on the paint surface as it stains paint. Keep wiping the area being worked on with a damp cloth. As each section is completed, wipe off with the cloth and dry with a piece of clean towelling or very soft cotton. Run your fingers over the surface and feel the difference. Using this process you are polishing the surface of the paint to create a beautiful silken smooth surface.

The sanding should be as even as possible. In effect a layer of paint is being removed and so the more even the sanding the more smooth the eventual finish will be. In particular, the edges of the piece should be wet-sanded carefully. To do this take a tiny edge of the sandpaper and gingerly wet-sand the edges so that the wood does not break through.

Fine swirl marks often left by wet-sanding are difficult to avoid. A truly fine and perfect surface is

WET-SANDING

1. For wet-sanding (or tuffbacking) carefully sand with 400 wet and dry sandpaper using a circular motion. Keep wiping off the scum with a damp cloth. When finished, wash down and dry thoroughly. 2. Make a bob from a piece of washed cotton 15 x 15 cm wrapped loosely around a ball of upholstery wadding. 3. Wipe the paint surface with tack cloth. Dip the bob into a small amount of bleached white shellac. 4. Draw the bob across the paint surface in straight, even strokes. 5. Lightly scour away any ridges with a scouring pad.

hard to achieve and it will only come with much practice and patience. Take your time when preparing pieces; remember there is no short cut to perfection in these finishes.

When the wet-sanding is completed wash with clean water to remove any scum left from the paint. Dry the piece and hold to the light to make sure there are no remaining patches that need attention. The piece is now ready to be isolated.

CHECKLIST
1. The paint surface should be very carefully wet-sanded. There should be no paint ridges, brush strokes or gritty patches remaining.
2. All paint scum should be washed off the paint surface using clean water and cloths.
3. The paint surface must not have water left on it nor become saturated with water.

ISOLATING

The purpose of isolating is to provide a surface for the antiquing glaze. In addition to the extra fine qualities imparted to the piece by wet-sanding, isolating provides a slick, non-porous surface over which the antiquing glaze will be applied. Every piece must be wet-sanded and isolated otherwise the glaze will be absorbed by the porous paint in an uneven, ugly fashion. Isolating, performed with shellac, also provides a barrier between the prepared paint surface and the antiquing glaze so that if necessary, the antiquing glaze may be removed. The antiquing glaze may be reapplied a number of times or until the best result is achieved.

Materials:

- ✦ *Bleached white shellac*
- ✦ *Rubber bands*
- ✦ *Small tin*
- ✦ *Clean soft cotton*
- ✦ *Upholstery cotton wadding*

Method: A bob is the most frequently used tool for applying an isolating coat. A bob eliminates all brush strokes leaving few, if any ridges.

To make your own bob take a piece of washed pure cotton that is smooth and free of texture. Cut into a square, the size of which will be determined by the size of the piece to be isolated. For a large sideboard, the bob would obviously require a large piece of fabric. Conversely, a smaller bob is sufficient for ornaments and other easy-to-handle pieces. Take a small piece of upholstery cotton wadding and place in the centre of the piece of cotton. Pull the cotton up loosely around the wadding and secure it with a rubber band. Make sure the cotton is not pulled too tightly around the wadding. The bob should be soft and pliable. Always keep two or three bobs handy in case the cotton breaks open.

Stir the shellac and pour a small amount into a tin. Carefully load the bob into the shellac about halfway up the side of the bob. Pull the bob over the side of the tin to scrape off excess shellac. Overloading of the bob is dangerous as heavy accumulations of shellac on the paint surface will not dry and leave ridges which will have to be eliminated later.

Wipe the surface with the tack cloth and then draw the loaded bob across the surface of the piece in a straight line. Each sweep should overlap with the last. As you work your way across the piece the cotton wadding will become saturated with shellac and it will not need as much re-loading as initially. For fine carving or raised areas use a No. 6 bright.

When the piece is completely isolated leave to dry for approximately twenty minutes. Then run a hand over the surface to make sure it is perfectly dry and apply a second coat to create a perfect seal. If little ridges start appearing where the shellac has been applied too heavily, damp a cloth with a little methylated spirits and carefully work over the ridges on wet and sticky places or scour gently with a scouring pad. This should remove any excess but if not properly done may create an even greater mess. If this does occur, don't despair! Wipe off the whole area of shellac with methylated spirits and start again. Do not be alarmed if the shellac appears to be streaky. This is unfortunately one of its properties. The streaking will be covered by the antiquing glaze.

When the two coats of shellac are dry, take a piece of scouring pad measuring approximately 5 cm x 4 cm and lightly abrade the shellac finish. Remove any ridges and make certain the surface is absolutely even. Once the surface is as smooth and even as possible it is ready for the antiquing glaze.

CHEATING ON PREPARATION

For those without the time to spend meticulously restoring, there is a quick way to achieve a good pre-antiquing finish. Although this method gives a perfectly acceptable finish to antiquing glaze stage, it is unsuitable as a base for two particular finishes, gilding and Japanese lacquer.

Method: Sand the piece, fill, then paint on an oil-based commercial primer and undercoat. This closes the grain, covers and protects the piece but it is impossible to achieve as fine a finish using this method as opposed to sealing with shellac.

Allow the piece to dry then lightly sand with 220 sandpaper and wipe with a cotton cloth and a tack cloth. Apply one coat of thinned down semi-gloss oil-based enamel paint and again dry overnight. Sand the piece lightly with 220 sandpaper; wipe with a cotton cloth and a tack cloth and apply a second coat of semi-gloss oil-based enamel paint. Once again, it is necessary to dry the piece overnight.

Providing the cover is opaque, the antiquing medium may be applied. If you make a mistake when applying the medium, it will simply wipe off the semi-gloss enamel in the same way it wipes off a surface that has been isolated with shellac.

An alternative cheat's method is to buy pieces that have already been prepared. Many department stores sell tables and chairs, coffee tables, bookcases and other pieces of furniture sprayed with a finish generally referred to as 'lacquer'. In the majority of cases,

the hard work has already been done by the manufacturer on these pieces and the antiquing medium can be applied almost immediately.

Pre-lacquered pieces are generally inexpensive and provide suitable working models. For example, see below, the white table and chairs with simple geometric pattern and antiqued with two colours using basic techniques. Also see page 15, a red coffee table with a black glaze applied with a graining tool. Many pieces can be bought pre-prepared and decorative finishes then simply applied.

Above, a white table and chairs bought from a chainstore. Right, the wonderful after-effect, a stippled blue glaze with alternate sections of the star dragged in yellow.

3

ANTIQUING GLAZES

A selection of trays is transformed into beautiful decorative and useful pieces using a range of the basic antiquing techniques described on the following pages.

AT LAST YOU HAVE REACHED the stage when you can apply an antiquing glaze to give a unique character to your chosen piece. This is the operation you have been working towards over many gruelling and painstaking hours of preparation. The antiquing glaze comprises the colour and texture that will transform your carefully prepared piece from a pumpkin to a glorious coach. These finishes sprang from the Venetian cabinetmakers' efforts to simulate Japanese and Chinese lacquer. Using the materials available in Europe — coach paint, copal varnish, shellac and other paints — a range of new finishes was developed. Over the intervening centuries, specialists working in this field have added and refined the repertoire and developed new tools. Today there is an extensive variety of antiquing glaze finishes available.

ANTIQUING, THE MOST SATISFYING area of painted finishes, is the process of applying glazes to give a mellow, aged appearance. Rather than giving a 'brand new' old look, an array of antiquing techniques can be employed to create pieces which are not only visually beautiful, but sit comfortably next to objects which are centuries-old.

The antiquing glaze consists of a semi-transparent film of paint which is superimposed over an opaque, sealed surface. This medium is composed of japan paint (or oil-based flat paint), scumbling medium and mineral turpentine. Formulas are given here with each technique. While the surface may be any colour, the glaze must always be a deeper shade than the colour beneath. If, when preparing a piece for antiquing, you have not decided on the colour of the antiquing glaze, the surface may be prepared in any case with the customary five coats of paint — in either white or off-white. Any colour in an antiquing glaze will lie comfortably over this ground.

It is up to the painter to control the density or level of translucence of the glaze. It can be one colour, or a series of overglazes, built up from light to dark with some of the surface colour showing through to give an appearance of depth. The word 'glaze' does not refer to a high sheen, but to the actual depth of colour or colours gained on application.

There are two different methods of application. The negative technique involves applying a glaze, usually with an oxhair brush, then removing some of the glaze with tools — cloths, sponges, chamois or brushes. The positive technique is simply application with a brush or another tool such as a sponge.

Before you commence antiquing, it is most important that you have in front of you every item you will need.

Materials:

- ✦ *Full set of eight brushes*
- ✦ *Chamois*
- ✦ *Sponges*
- ✦ *Mineral turpentine*
- ✦ *Cotton cloths*
- ✦ *Kerosene*
- ✦ *Plant mister for kerosene*
- ✦ *Clean butchers' paper*

For a basic glaze, mix together one part japan paint (in a colour you have pre-mixed — see Colour Recipes chapter) and one part scumbling medium. Thin the mixture with mineral turpentine, as described in each of the following glazes. Be aware that paint has only a short time in which it can be worked. Scumbling medium enables you to leave the impression of a tool in the paint and it also slightly extends the drying time. With practice you will quickly establish how soon the paint sets up and when you must stop working it with a tool. If overworked, the antiquing glaze will take on an unattractive, coarse, bruised look.

During antiquing, never put any of your brushes directly into mineral turpentine as the drenched brush may flood the next glaze you perform. If the brushes seem to be becoming stiff, soften them by running them through a cloth which has been wrung out in mineral turpentine. When leaving a brush covered in antiquing glaze for more than five minutes, remember to wrap it in cling wrap so that the brush will not run the risk of becoming stiff.

Basic finishes individualise tin boxes bought at a supermarket. The finishes on each are as follows: top, negative stippling, spattering, negative dragging; middle, sponging, distressing, positive stippling; bottom; flotation dragging, chamois, provincial dragging.

Essential components of any antiquing glaze: paint, scumbling medium and mineral turpentine.

Provincial dragging. Load brush, remove excess paint, pull brush across the surface in a series of fine lines. Start and finish on the border of the tape. Add a negative stippled border and a positive stripe, as above.

PROVINCIAL DRAGGING

This is a positive glaze that gives an old look to chairs and country-style furniture.

Materials:

+ *One part japan paint*
+ *One part scumbling medium*
+ *2.5 cm fitch brush*

Method: Unless the composition is extremely thick, it may not be necessary to thin the glaze. The brush should be clean and dry for this finish. Load one side of the fitch very lightly into the glaze. Pull the brush across clean butchers' paper to remove some of the paint. When you see a series of fine lines forming, start working. Pull the brush across the chosen surface in a series of very fine, straight parallel lines. If the brush seems to be empty of paint, put more pressure on the handle and more paint will flow from the brush. However, the pressure from one end of the stroke to the other should be even. Allow the brush to come lightly off the end of the surface. This finish can be made to take on the appearance of fabric if, immediately after it is applied, a small, folded piece of cheesecloth is gently patted over the paint. Alternatively, create a harsh look by loading the brush heavily and pulling heavy lines across the surface.

NEGATIVE DRAGGING

Otherwise called dragging, this classic wall glaze is also extremely useful for the tops and sides of chests, tables and other pieces.

Materials:

+ *One part japan paint*
+ *One part scumbling medium*
+ *One part mineral turpentine*
+ *Oxhair brush*
+ *2.5 cm fitch brush*

Method: Hold a cotton cloth in your left hand. With the oxhair brush, quickly paint the glaze onto the object, taking care to make sure the cover is solid. Take the fitch and pull it through the paint in a straight line. Wipe off on the cloth and continue in parallel strokes until you have pulled the brush through the entire body of paint. Now go back over the surface and, using plenty of strength on the brush, work it harshly back and forth across the paint surface. If you want to achieve a softer appearance, work the brush gently backwards and forwards. The brush should be wiped off with the cotton cloth constantly to avoid redistributing the paint on the object. Do not sweep across the board more than three times. By then, the paint will be setting and it will be difficult to work.

FLOTATION DRAGGING

A beautiful, silken finish used on horizontal surfaces only, such as insets for tables and chest tops.

Materials:

+ *One part japan paint*
+ *One part scumbling medium*
+ *One part mineral turpentine*
+ *Kerosene*
+ *Nylon brush*
+ *2.5 cm fitch brush*

Method: Using the nylon brush, carefully coat the surface of your piece well with kerosene. Load the fitch brush carefully into the paint. Take off excess paint on butchers' paper and pull the brush gently across the top of the kerosene in a series of straight lines. Do not place pressure on the brush at this stage — it may pull the kerosene off, thereby stopping the

NEGATIVE DRAGGING

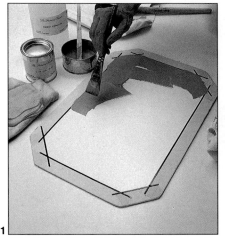
1

2

3

1. Paint on antiquing glaze with an oxhair brush. Pull the fitch brush through the glaze to create striping. 2. Wipe the brush with a clean cotton cloth after each stroke. 3. The result: negative dragging with a negative stippled border and a negative stripe.

FLOTATION DRAGGING

1

2

3

1. Paint on a good cover of kerosene. 2. Load the fitch brush with antiquing glaze and pull very lightly across the top of the kerosene. You may rework this once or twice. This is a fragile finish and may take some time to dry. 3. Flotation dragging centre, negative stippled border and negative stripe.

NEGATIVE STIPPLING

1

2

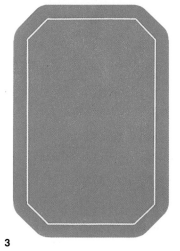
3

1. Quickly cover the board with glaze using an oxhair brush. 2. Pounce the stipple brush up and down to create brush marks, while also allowing light through from below. Keep even and keep moving the brush in a circular motion so that there are no straight lines. Quickly wipe paint off the brush after each pounce.

flotation process. Once the entire surface is covered, carefully work the brush backwards and forwards once or twice to smooth and blend the antiquing glaze. You will now see the kerosene starting to work on the paint, 'opening' it out so that the glaze will float and move slightly. This is a very fine, gossamer-like glaze which imparts an exquisite effect.

> **Warning:** When kerosene has been used as a base beneath an antiquing glaze, the object should be moved very carefully otherwise the glaze will run. A kerosene-based glaze takes up to forty-eight hours or more to dry (depending upon the weather).
>
> It is wise to keep the atmosphere and tools as free of dust as is possible when performing this finish as the glaze attracts dust while it is being performed. Because kerosene causes paint to become very fragile, there is always the additional risk that some of the paint will be dragged off by the brush during application of the first varnish coat. To overcome this the first coat of varnish should be thinned using equal proportions of varnish and mineral turpentine. (See Chapter 5.)

A selection of finished boards using basic antiquing glazes in shades of blue.

paint. The finished surface should end up as an even, smoothly patterned surface with a little of the background colour showing through.

NEGATIVE STIPPLING

In the USA this is referred to as pouncing.

Materials:

+ *One part japan paint*
+ *One part scumbling medium*
+ *One oxhair brush*
+ *One part mineral turpentine*
+ *One stipple brush*

Method: Load the oxhair brush with the glaze and quickly coat the surface. Holding a piece of cotton cloth in the left hand and the stippling brush in the right, pounce the brush down onto the glaze at an angle perpendicular to the surface. The brush must not be applied in straight lines. It should move back and forth over the surface and be turned in the air before each application so that the texture on the glaze remains irregular. If the brush turns on the paint surface, swirl marks may appear in the glaze.

Each time the brush is raised from the surface it must be wiped with the cloth to remove some of the

POSITIVE STIPPLING

Materials:

+ *One part japan paint*
+ *One part scumbling medium*
+ *One part mineral turpentine*
+ *Stipple brush*

Method: Load the stipple brush into the glaze, just onto the hair tips. Alternatively, wipe the stipple brush over a lightly loaded oxhair brush. The stipple brush must then be rubbed vigorously over butchers' paper to make sure that there is an absolutely even distribution on the hairs. The secret of this finish is that the stipple brush is minimally, evenly loaded.

Holding the brush at least 10 cm from the board, pounce it up and down onto the surface. Try to turn the brush in the air so that the shape of the pounce mark changes with every application. (If the brush is turned on the surface, undesirable swirl marks will appear.) The application should be as even as possible and without any appearance of straight lines. Think in the form of a drift of clouds scudding across the sky, or a formation of stone running through marble and keep pouncing irregularly so that there are no straight lines. This is a more difficult technique than negative stippling. It takes time to master an even, consistent stippled finish.

POSITIVE STIPPLING

1

2

3

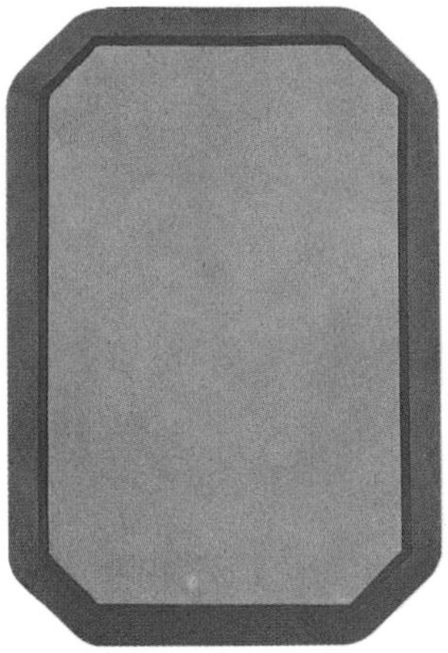

4

SPONGING

1

2

3

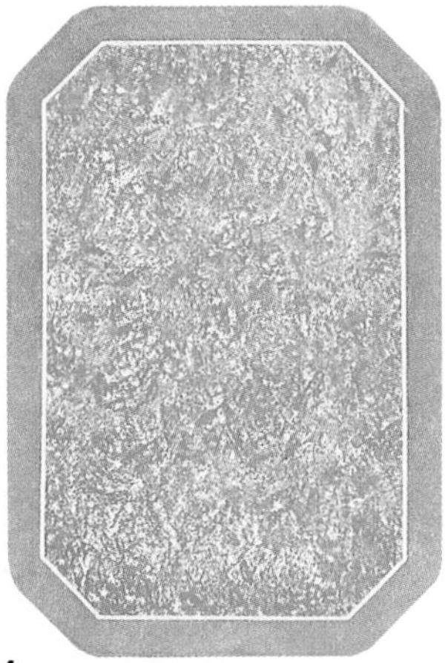

4

CHAMOIS

1

2

3

4

SPONGING

Materials:

- ✦ *One part japan paint*
- ✦ *One part scumbling medium*
- ✦ *One part mineral turpentine*
- ✦ *Natural sea sponges (not synthetic!)*

Method: Only natural sponges will impart the soft, mottled appearance achieved using this technique. Synthetic sponges are undesirable tools that create harsh, unattractive outlines. Sponging is a traditional wall glazing technique which may be applied successfully, positively or negatively. The sponge creates a stone-like texture not dissimilar to that of lapis lazuli and marble. It is most effective on larger surfaces. The above recipe uses only a small proportion of mineral turpentine. If you prefer a thin, washy glaze, add more mineral turpentine to the mixture.

Firstly, wring out the sea sponge in water so that it is malleable and easy to use. No water should be left in the sponge. Lightly load the sponge into the glaze and then take off on clean butchers' paper. As with other antiquing glazes, the tool must be properly unloaded. Heavy globules of paint in holes in the sponge may suddenly appear and ruin the application. This finish, performed properly, can boast an 'even unevenness'.

Wearing surgical gloves (household rubber gloves tend to leave brilliant fingerprint impressions in paint), hold the sponge lightly and apply the glaze to the board in a drift-like fashion, allowing negative space (the background) to show through so that you have a definition of colour. If you want to blend the harder edges slightly, use a clean sponge which has been wrung out in water, or a stipple brush to blend gently. Although the finish should be subtle, a softer finish can be created by thinning the glaze.

Materials:

- ✦ *One part japan paint*
- ✦ *One part scumbling medium*
- ✦ *Six parts or more mineral turpentine*

Method: In this case you would need to wring out the sponge lightly after dipping it in the antiquing glaze. This combination gives a runny glaze unsuitable for use on walls or any vertical surface.

For a very graphic sponged appearance, apply the antiquing glaze in a thick mixture. Or, create the appearance of fur by using a negative technique, as follows:

Materials:

- ✦ *One part japan paint*
- ✦ *One part scumbling medium*
- ✦ *One part mineral turpentine*
- ✦ *Oxhair brush*
- ✦ *Stipple brush*

Method: Quickly apply the paint with the oxhair brush. Stipple all over to remove the brush strokes and start texturing with the damp sponge. For an unusual furry look, place the sponge on the glaze and move it sideways in a varying semi-circular motion. Once the process is completed, rinse the sponge in mineral turpentine, then in soap and hot water.

CHAMOIS

This is a very useful technique which forms the basis of many stone and marble finishes. It can also simulate the look of crushed velvet or parchment. The process is always negative as it is not aesthetically satisfactory to apply paint with a chamois.

Materials:

- ✦ *One part scumbling medium*
- ✦ *One part mineral turpentine*
- ✦ *One part japan paint*
- ✦ *Oxhair brush*
- ✦ *Stipple brush*
- ✦ *Pure chamois*

Method: Cut each piece of chamois into pieces roughly 15 cm x 15 cm and wring out in water exactly as for sponges. When using chamois it is wise to have more than one piece on hand as the chamois does not give the effect you desire if it is clogged with paint.

Chamois is used to create stone-like marble looks. If marble finishes are of interest to you, start observing pieces of marble and note the flow, drift and shape of the formed stones. If you want to create a stone-like appearance as the basis of an impressionistic marble finish, first paint on the antiquing glaze with an oxhair brush. Stipple very quickly to remove the brush strokes and having studied stone shapes, fold the chamois in a geometric stone-like shape and

Margin captions

1. Pounce a lightly loaded stipple brush over the board. 2. The brush is reloaded using the oxhair brush. 3. The stipple brush is carefully off-loaded before stippling once more. 4. Positive stipple centre, negative stipple border and positive stripe.

1. Wring out sponge in water. 2. Load sponge into antiquing glaze and take off on paper. 3. Unload over board in a series of controlled pats. 4. Sponge centre, negative stipple border and negative stripe.

1. Quickly paint on the glaze. 2. Quickly stipple to remove any brush strokes. 3. Wring chamois out in water, roll into a sausage and roll across the board. 4. Chamois centre, negative stipple border and positive stripe.

For the fireboard above and right, a trompe l'oeil vase was painted onto a basic black background. (Photo courtesy Mode magazine.)

The chintz flowers were cut out and pasted on and the fireboard was placed in the fireplace, ready for use throughout the summer months. (Photo courtesy Mode magazine.)

DISTRESSING

1. The surface has been sanded carefully with 220 sandpaper, and a negative stripe has been applied using 6mm masking tape. Paint on the contrast colour. 2. Using either 220 sandpaper, steel wool or 400 wet and dry sandpaper, or all three, create areas of wear on the surface. 3. The finished distressed surface.

impress it on the paint surface. Lift and re-fold into a different stone-like shape and repeat the impression so a drift of stones appears across the surface. Once the first drift is completed, run the drifts off it until the surface is finished. Try to control the amount of paint that is removed with each stone. If you are deliberately able to change the amount removed, leaving a little more here, or less there, the finished appearance will be more realistic. (See page 143)

A 'crushed velvet' look is useful for backgrounds. Roll the chamois diagonally into a sausage and roll it quickly and diagonally across the surface. Chamois is cleaned in the same way as sponges.

DISTRESSING

Materials:

+ *400 wet and dry sandpaper*
+ *220 sandpaper*
+ *Steel wool*

This technique produces a provincial, naive effect on country-style furniture. It is also an extremely useful means for ageing surfaces. The normal procedure is to apply three to four coats of base colour, following the normal steps as described in the preparation chapter, sanding with 220 paper or steel wool, depending upon the type of piece and the colour of the base coat, and finally applying one or two coats of a different colour. It is not necessary to apply an isolating coat of shellac between these coats. The surface is distressed after the normal drying time.

Before commencing distressing, study the piece,

noting the areas likely to be the most worn, for example, the areas around handles, edges and corners. In these spots the wood can be made to break through the paint. Furthermore it is likely that the entire piece will have 'aged' and therefore the whole paint surface must be worked on with distressing materials so that some of the under colour comes through. For this process the above three materials may be carefully used in conjunction with each other. On a small box, for example, 220 sandpaper would first be used, followed by steel wool. If using 400 wet and dry sandpaper be careful as this quickly removes the paint. If you happen to remove too much colour, simply apply another coat and distress again the next day or after twenty-four hours.

AGEING WITH WAX AND JAPAN PAINT

This technique is particularly useful for ageing picture frames and carved surfaces. It is often used over a painted decoration such as a naive painting on a box or chest. When the antiquing and naive painting are completed the piece is further aged with wax mixed with paint.

This medium is also used successfully on carved chairs — and in conjunction with rottenstone for an exaggerated aged effect. When ageing with wax and japan paint remember that the surface should not be sealed prior to application as the paint surface should be slightly porous and more readily able to hold the wax and paint. Colours most frequently used are

A papier-mâché rooster looks almost antique with a distressed and waxed finish.

earth tones such as raw or burnt umber. Burnt tends towards warm, reddish tones and raw towards green, cool shades.

Materials:

- ✦ **One part carnauba wax**
- ✦ **.12 to .25 part Burnt or Raw Umber**
- ✦ **Palette knife**
- ✦ **Stipple brush**

Method: Place the wax on a piece of parchment or wax paper of four thicknesses and thoroughly blend it with a palette knife. It should be very creamy with no residual granules of wax left. If granules are left, they will melt when applied to the piece, giving an uneven mottled effect. Add the paint and mix together thoroughly. The medium is best applied to the piece in a positive stipple. Load the stipple brush into the wax medium. Carefully rub the brush off on butchers' paper until the loading is even. Pounce onto the piece. As paint and wax do not set up and dry quickly this medium can be reworked as necessary.

A heavier, more textured aged look is achieved by applying the medium with an oxhair brush and then stippling the surface with a clean brush. If the surface is carved, an alternative means of ageing is to apply the medium (allow some days for drying), buff the piece off with a soft cloth, spoon on rottenstone and pounce into the interstices of the carving with a clean brush. When the excess rottenstone is brushed off an old grey finish is left.

Warning: When using rottenstone it is wise to wear a cheap mask as fine powder can be inhaled and damage the lungs.

AGEING WITH WAX AND JAPAN PAINT

1. Smooth wax out with a palette knife. 2. Mix in either burnt or raw umber. 3. Load stipple brush and then unload on clean butchers' paper. 4. Stipple onto surface.

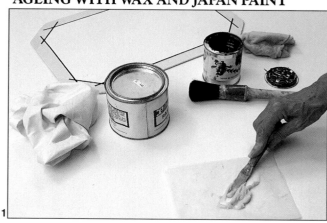

To restore this whitewood chest of drawers, pink paint was stippled over white and spattered with aniline dye. The design was imposed, the piece flat-varnished and then waxed.

SPATTERING

Materials:

- ✦ *Cheap brush (2.5 cm)*
- ✦ *Hammer*
- ✦ *Chinese cleaver*
- ✦ *Chopping board*
- ✦ *Kerosene in a plant mister*
- ✦ *One part japan paint*
- ✦ *Four parts mineral turpentine*

Method: Spattering, normally used at the end of the antiquing process, adds depth to a finish. If a finish appears too dull and needs some extra interest, or if it is too bright and garish and needs to be toned down, spattering is applied. Carved surfaces are also highlighted by a spatter finish, and irregularities in antiquing glazes can generally be disguised by spattering. Mistakes can be rectified by spattering the blemish with the same colour.

Using masking tape, mask the brush tip about 1.5 cm above the ferrule, leaving a small space. Mask again around the tips of the hairs to hold them together. Lay the taped brush down on the cutting board, place the cleaver across the space between the two pieces of masking tape and strike the cleaver quickly and forcefully with the hammer. One blow should sever the end bristles from the brush. Flick the bristles of the brush to remove any excess hairs not already released.

For this operation, there is no need to add scumbling medium to the japan paint unless it is already mixed with the colour you wish to use. In this case it is perfectly acceptable to thin down this mix, using it as the spatter medium.

Load the brush in the paint and then hold the brush on its side and pull over clean butchers' paper, turning from side to side and placing a lot of pressure on the brush. If the brush is overloaded the paint will drip down the ferrule and splash onto the finish. (If this does happen, place a cotton bud or piece of fine cotton in the centre of the drip to soak up some of the paint. If the edges are very round and symmetrical, roughen them a little, removing any excess paint and then cover by running a very fine spatter over the imperfection on the finish.)

Using a separate brush for each colour, load and unload the brush as above, hold it on its side in your left hand and place the thumb of your right hand on the ferrule of the brush. Pull your right index finger up over the hairs of the brush and spatter the paint. Keep moving the brush around in a circular motion to prevent the application being too heavy in one area. Load the brush with the first colour and run a spatter over the board. Load with the second colour and run another fine spatter over the first. You may wish to intensify this spatter in say, the corners of the piece. The next colour should follow. You may wish to add a different dimension by taking a thinned-down fourth colour.

Composition:

- ✦ *One part japan paint*
- ✦ *Eight parts mineral turpentine*

Before using this mixture, test it on newspaper. Load the brush, pull out a little on newspaper then hold over the board and hit solidly with a hammer. This will create big, open splodgy spatters. An interesting effect can be achieved by spraying kerosene from a plant mister onto the already spattered surface, followed by the application (spattering) of one or two more colours. The kerosene will cause the colours to reticulate slightly. You may also wish to hold the

A simple antiquing glaze painted on the edges of a decorative screen.

SPATTERING

1

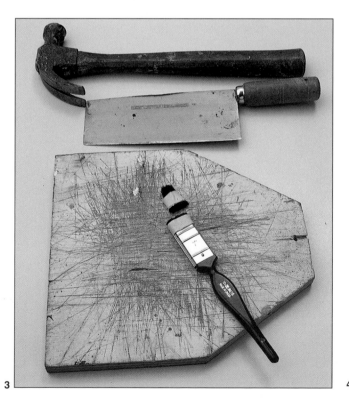

2

3

4

5

1. Tape the brush so that when cut, the hairs will be approximately 12-19mm long. 2. Place cleaver between the two sets of tape and bring hammer down sharply. 3. The brush should now be evenly cut and the tape can be removed. 4. Load brush with runny paint and pull out on paper to remove excess paint. Hold brush in left hand, place right thumb on ferrule and pull index finger from the bottom to the top of the bristles. Keep moving the brush in a circular motion to eliminate straight lines. 5. Spatter centre, negative stipple border and negative stripe.

The above fireboard has a green marble border painted onto cardboard. A green spatter leaves the imprint of foliage on a sienna background.

A pair of standard handturned wooden candlesticks is transformed with a blue spatter finish over a white background, and silver leaf trims.

board sideways a little to move the paint around. Be careful, as the finish may be easily ruined by moving the board around too much. If you use kerosene, wait a little longer for it to dry. Varnish the surface with a mixture of one part varnish and one part mineral turpentine for the first coat.

Warning: When applying an antiquing glaze make sure that any glaze which has fallen onto an area not already antiqued is wiped off. Do not attempt to paint the glaze over this and then apply the tool to that area. You will find that the glaze which has been spilled, or left from the first application, will show through the antiquing glaze painted over it.

Always watch for this when working and keep cleaning the areas not already antiqued. This is a situation where the isolating coats of shellac are useful.

Hairs which fall into a glaze can be removed by turning a piece of masking tape in half and gingerly placing it, sticky-side-out on top of the hair and quickly pulling it away. Usually this will remove the hair without damaging the finish.

Remember that when you are mixing a colour for the antiquing glaze, strain before mixing with scumbling medium. If the scumbling medium becomes lumpy or forms a skin on the surface, it should be strained.

Do not use a tack cloth which has been applied to dark colours on a pale colour. Once a tack cloth has been used on a dark surface, keep it for that purpose. Ideally, you should have three tack cloths on hand at once: one for dark, one for medium and one for light colours.

It is most important that the application of the antiquing glaze is quickly stippled to remove the brush strokes when it is first applied. A badly executed painted finish usually shows brush strokes or tool marks. Observers should not be able to remark upon the sponge, chamois or brush marks. The tools used to create a finish should remain a secret!

Top, a very simple finish applied to a reproduction chair. Deep cream paint was coated on and an even deeper shade was rubbed into the mouldings on the chair. A blue stripe was added for subtle detail, above.

4

STRIPING AND IMPOSING A DESIGN

ONCE A PIECE of furniture or a small object has taken an antiquing glaze, the finish can often require some additional detail. One of the most useful and surprisingly simple means of achieving this is to apply striping. A stripe can be applied to a tray, to the legs of a chair or as a band on the outside edge of a table. Striping adds extra dimension to a piece as well as completing its final appearance. Likewise, a geometric design, or flowers and figures can successfully complement the antiquing glaze. The design is imposed using a simple method which is easy to learn. Follow the directions provided in this chapter and your design will appear magically before you.

POSITIVE AND NEGATIVE STRIPING are extremely useful decorative techniques which can be used on either period or contemporary pieces. Striping on contemporary pieces is usually stylised and geometric whilst on period furniture it can be more free-flowing.

NEGATIVE STRIPING

Take a sample board and place masking tape 2.5 cm wide around the outside edge. Place narrow tape 3 mm wide on the inside of the 2.5 cm tape. These are butted right up beside each other so that there is no space between the two tapes. Paint antiquing glaze onto the negative space inside the narrow tape. When the glaze is set remove the wide tape and remove straggling ends on the inside narrow tape with a sharp knife. Apply the glaze to the outside edge. Allow the glaze to dry for two or three hours and then carefully remove the inside black tape. The clean negative space showing should now form a stripe.

POSITIVE STRIPING

Positive striping is always superimposed on top of the completed antiquing glaze. Take a sample board and mask with 2.5 cm tape around the outside edge. The antiquing glaze is then applied to the inside negative space and when set (two hours), lift the outside tape and apply another antiquing glaze to the outside edge. Twenty-four hours later the board should be isolated with a coat of shellac using an oxhair brush. (See page 51.)

The antiquing medium should be isolated with shellac first so that the masking tape used for striping will not pull off any of the finish. Isolating a piece with shellac allows it to be worked on almost immediately, but do not use a bob in this case as this may pull off the antiquing glaze.

When isolating with shellac at this final stage, the streaks created will be absorbed by varnish only. Thus, if the finish is simply to be waxed rather than varnished, do not use an isolating coat of shellac. Instead apply a coat of flat varnish, dry for twenty-four hours and proceed with the striping. Take extreme care not to pull off any paint with the masking tape. Buy special low-tack tape for this purpose.

To isolate, place a small amount of shellac in a tin and, using an oxhair brush, lightly load and apply in gentle sweeps to the antiquing glaze. Do not paint back and forth as the shellac dries instantly. Carefully pull the brush across the piece, distributing the shellac as evenly as possible. Use one coat only and do not abrade with a scouring pad. Now that the finish is protected masking tape can be laid down.

A piece of 6 mm masking tape should be placed immediately down over the join of the two antiquing mediums. Mask-in this tape using extra tape on either side. Lift the centre tape to reveal the space in which to paint the stripe. This negative space should then be abraded with 220 sandpaper in order to knock down the ridges created by the join. Finally wipe off with a cotton cloth and tack cloth and ram the edges of the masking tape down carefully with a thumb nail.

The paint is then mixed to a suitable consistency. (Scumbling medium is not necessary but if the colour used has scumbling medium in it it will not make any difference to the stripe). It should not be too thick as it may form ridges against the masking tape. Conversely, if it is too thin it will seep beneath the masking tape and create a fuzzy edge.

Apply one coat, wait for half an hour and apply a second coat. As soon as the paint sets up remove the masking tape. Remember that masking tape should not be left on overnight as it may pull off the finish. When the masking tape is taken off the strip will appear opaque against the finish.

It is unusual to require three coats of paint. As the third coat tends to pull off the previous two it can be applied freehand if necessary the next day.

A good example using masking tape is seen on the table and chairs with a blue and yellow finish. (See page 27.) The table and chairs were bought in a department store and already had a white lacquer finish. Two antiquing glazes were applied to that finish without any preparation except an initial cleansing wipe with a cloth soaked in mineral turpentine.

The design was laid out geometrically, using a hard pencil and large ruler. Once the table was measured into quarters, eighths and sixteenths the points for the star were joined. Using 12 mm masking tape, the design was masked in and a negative dragging was applied to alternate sections of the star using a lemon antiquing glaze. The masking

NEGATIVE STRIPING

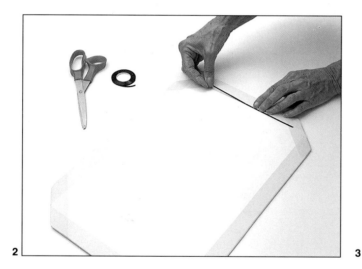

1. First lay in the masking tape around the outside edge. 2. Lay the second tape which will create the stripe up to the edge of the first tape all the way around the board. 3. When the centre space has been antiqued, carefully cut off the ends of the narrow tape and remove the outside masking tape. 4. Stipple the outside edge. 5. When paint has set up (about 20-30 minutes) remove narrow tape to reveal the stripe.

A basic example of the use of quick finishes, this fireboard was easily made using a piece of cardboard which is striped, using 2.5cm masking tape. The simple illustration of geese was painted over the top.

tape was removed and twenty-four hours later the lemon sections were isolated with shellac applied with an oxhair brush.

Masking tape was laid on to allow antiquing on the other part of the star. A blue negative stipple was applied, followed by texturing with a sponge. Having lifted the latter masking tape the table was left for twenty-four hours, after which the blue section of the star was isolated with shellac. Finally, the whole star was masked in and a negative stipple applied to the outside edge of the table.

The chairs were finished in a much more hap-hazard fashion. The negative stripes were laid in by eye and 6 mm masking tape and the chairs were antiqued using blue glaze in a negative stipple. Once the tape was removed, the yellow stripe was carefully painted in freehand.

IMPOSING A DESIGN

Imposing a design is the most useful technique for placing a design on an antiqued piece. The method explained in this chapter enables those who cannot draw to paint sophisticated, naive or simple designs on almost anything.

Materials:

- ✦ *Artists' transfer paper (Saral USA) available in Red, Blue, Yellow and White*
- ✦ *2H pencil*
- ✦ *Tracing paper*

Method: A design using artists' transfer paper should only be imposed on a piece which has been sealed — either with a coat of flat varnish which has dried for twenty-four hours or with a coat of shellac applied with an oxhair brush and dried for twenty minutes. The reason for isolating at this stage is that if the chalk in the artists' transfer paper comes off on undesired areas of the finish it can be removed easily with mineral turpentine. It is extremely difficult to remove chalk from a surface which has not been isolated.

When applying a design to a smallish piece — for example a table top or a tray — cut a template to fit the piece. Having decided on the design (postcards, wrapping paper and posters provide an exhaustive source of ideas), place the template over the design, centre it and secure with masking tape. Carefully trace the design using a 2H pencil. When this is completed, place the template on the antiqued surface and secure it with masking tape. Watch that the masking tape does not pull off any of the finish.

Take a piece of artists' transfer paper and test that it is right side down by running the sharp point of a pencil across one section. If colour does not come off, it is the wrong side down. This simple test can save hours of fruitless time spent tracing a design back onto the tracing paper rather than onto the object.

Slip the artists' carbon beneath the tracing paper and trace over the design, occasionally lifting one corner of the tracing paper to check that the design is being transferred. The carbon leaves a very fine mark and if the pressure is not applied heavily enough, the traced image may be difficult to make out.

Once the tracing is completed, lift the paper and look at the transferred design. Now it is up to you to take the colours you have chosen and paint in the design. For a surprisingly simple and straight forward process, the result is usually excellent.

POSITIVE STRIPING

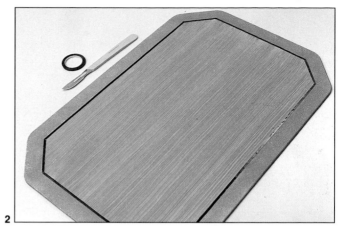

5

1. Using an oxhair brush, apply an isolating coat of shellac before performing a positive stripe. 2. Place a narrow tape over the join. 3. Now mask in the narrow tape with masking tape. 4. Remove narrow tape, sand the exposed area with 220 sandpaper to ensure that it is smooth. Run a thumbnail along the edges of the masking tape before painting in the stripe using a sable brush. 5. Remove the masking tape carefully to show the positive stripe.

IMPOSING A DESIGN

1. A template of tracing paper is cut to fit the piece and an isolating coat of shellac is applied to the finish. The template is placed on the finish. Artists' transfer paper is slipped underneath and the design traced on. 2. The design is painted in using a sable brush.

5

DYES AND OVERGLAZES

MANY FINISHES REQUIRE an extra application of colour or texture. The recipes in this chapter will prove invaluable for this purpose. Aniline dyes, because of their translucency, impart a subtle appearance of use and mellowness without too much heaviness — perfect for the process of ageing a piece. Japan paint is also used for ageing and you will find that asphaltum, when used as an overglaze, adds additional depth to a finish. The varnish finishes containing bronze powder add lustre to final finishes. Indeed, any finish which appears too bright or too dull can be completely transformed using the following recipes.

ANILINE DYE

ANILINE DYES, normally bought in powder form, expand from only a tiny sprinkling into surprisingly large quantities. Don't be misled by this seemingly harmless powder — aniline dyes are extremely toxic and should not come into contact with skin or be inhaled. Although a complete range of dye colours is produced for the professional dyeing industry, the earth tones similar to raw and burnt umber are generally used as antiquing mediums.

Composition:

+ *One-eighth teaspoon aniline dye*
+ *60 mls methylated spirits*
+ *60 mls shellac*

Method: Place the dye in the bottom of a small jar and pour in a tiny amount of methylated spirits. When the dye is dissolved, pour in the rest of the methylated spirits and the shellac. Combine and immediately place a piece of cling wrap over the top of the mixture to prevent evaporation. (If the spirits dry out in the jar the dye will still retain its main constituents. Rejuvenate the mixture by adding methylated spirits and shellac, as required.)

Aniline dye is often referred to as a 'fugitive' material. This means that the colour can suddenly disappear and shellac is used as a fixative to prevent this occurring. If the dye disappears after one application it is necessary to add more shellac to the mixture to fix the dye. This fugitive reaction can also occur when methylated spirits evaporates in a bottle, leaving the dye mixture. When this happens more shellac and methylated spirits should be added.

By far the most successful method of applying aniline dye to a piece is spattering. Stippling is also possible but as the shellac base of the mixture is quick-drying it is difficult to manipulate. Shellac-based mixtures will also pull off an isolating coat of shellac. Therefore if you choose to stipple on the dye, the antiquing glaze beneath may not be isolated and the dye must be stippled directly onto the finish. If a mistake is made while stippling, the stipple will have to be wiped off with methylated spirits without removing the fragile antiquing glaze beneath.

Spattering is the safer, simpler and more aesthetic-ally pleasing way in which to use these dyes. For a fine, soft finish, load the brush lightly, pull it out on clean butchers' paper and start spattering. For a heavy spatter load the brush heavily, removing only a small amount and, having first tried this over newspaper, hit the brush with a hammer to distribute large, open blobs on the piece. Carry on spattering many times over for a crusty, aged look.

AGEING WITH PAINT

Another medium for ageing can be made by suspending a small amount of burnt or raw umber in flat varnish. This mixture does not quite achieve the translucent quality of aniline dyes but it is particularly useful as a substitute. It can be spattered and since it is turpentine based it can be applied to an isolated surface in a positive or negative stipple.

+ *One tablespoon flat varnish*
+ *Mineral turpentine, quantity as desired*
+ *Half teaspoon Burnt or Raw Umber*

SPATTER

Spatter makes an excellent final antiquing finish. Any colour can be used to finish off an antiquing glaze. For example, a pale blue sponged finish can be complemented with a spatter in a darker tone of blue and a slightly 'blued' white. The range of colour combinations used in a spatter as a final antiquing finish is virtually limitless.

In cases where much hard work has been done to produce a good sponged or stippled finish it is most probably unnecessary to spatter the piece. Remember that spatter in this instance is an addition to the main antiquing glaze. It is a means of adding more depth and interest to the finish, not necessarily a finish itself. (See Chapter 3.)

OVERGLAZES

Much interest and depth can be added to antiquing glazes by adding overglazes to the final finish. One coat may be sufficient or you can build up different coats for a rich, deep, interesting finish.

+ *One part paint*
+ *Nine parts mineral turpentine*

Detail of the dresser shown overleaf, illustrating the rich effect created by stippling and reticulating asphaltum over a red base. The panel and supporting base of the dresser are in oxidised Dutch metal.

Method: If you feel nervous about this strength of mixture, apply an isolating coat of shellac over the existing finish. Try to do this carefully so that not too many streak marks are left on top of the finish. Ideally, it is best to take your courage in both hands and apply the overglaze without isolating first.

Paint the overglaze quickly onto the finish and stipple to remove brush strokes. Crumple a piece of tissue paper and dab it in a drift-like, uneven motion; or dampen a sponge in water, wring it out and apply to give the overglaze a dimpled, cloudy appearance. Cotton T-shirting or cheesecloth can also be used.

In order to add depth to the finish, you can keep building up a series of glazes. In this case do not isolate between coats as a system of brush strokes will build up and show through the varnish. A glaze in white is always very effective and works well over light and middle value colours. Conversely, black works successfully over dark colours, particularly dark green and purple. Alternatively, you may wish to build up a series of colours.

PEARLISED FINISH

To obtain a thin pearlised finish over an antiquing glaze, simply mix some pearlescent powder into the varnish, using approximately the following quantities:

+ *One tablespoon*   + *Six tablespoons*
  pearlescent powder   *varnish*

Method: This finish is usually most successful if high gloss varnish is used. First mix a few drops of varnish into the powder to make sure that it is all absorbed, then pour in the rest of the varnish. The mixture must be stirred constantly to keep the powder floating evenly. This mixture will keep for a long time if cling wrap is placed onto the surface of the liquid. The lovely mother-of-pearl qualities imparted by this mixture sit comfortably on most colours, though especially over pale to middle toned blues, pinks and greens.

Gold and silver bronzing powders may be used in the same way as above, suspended to the same formula. Be careful when mixing these powders as they are made of fine ground metal and may cause injury if inhaled.

LACE TORTOISESHELL

This is a rich, fluid overglaze made from tar and often referred to as lace tortoiseshell. The asphaltum is available from specialty art shops. Use enough mineral turpentine to thin the mixture if it appears viscous. Asphaltum's consistency often varies but for this finish it should be thin enough to paint onto a horizontal surface without running.

Composition:

+ *65 mls scumbling medium (omit for horizontal surfaces)*
+ *65 mls asphaltum*
+ *Mineral turpentine as required*
+ *Plant mister filled with mineral turpentine*

Method: Store mixture in a screw-top jar with cling wrap placed immediately over the surface of the mixture. For a tortoiseshell effect the background should be cream, but this glaze works especially well when laid over a dark red base. Paint the glaze on and stipple to remove any brush strokes. Put some mineral turpentine in a plant mister and spray into the air immediately above the mixture allowing the turpentine to fall softly into the finish. This disperses the asphaltum in a fascinating process.

The asphaltum may take much longer to dry than paint, depending on the type of asphaltum used. Australian asphaltum dries quite quickly, usually in forty-eight hours, but American asphaltum can take up to two weeks. Be careful to isolate with two coats of shellac using an oxhair brush before varnishing as the varnish may pull off the asphaltum.

Warning: Do not inhale any fumes from this mixture as it contains cobalt drier which is very toxic. When preparing and using it, wear a mask and make certain that the work area is well ventilated.

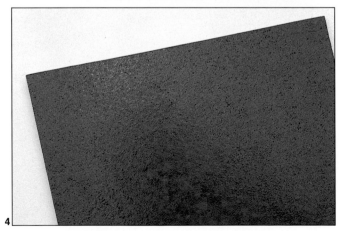

1. The board has been prepared in the usual fashion. The asphaltum is painted on.
2. Stipple to remove brush strokes. 3. Spray lightly with mineral turpentine two or three times. Make sure that the spray is a light mist. Watch the glaze open up. Remember to isolate with shellac before varnishing. 4. The finished board — asphaltum overglaze. Right, asphaltum overglaze makes a dramatic contrast in a plate laid on a green marbled table.

VARNISHING

Varnish is the final coat that gives protection to painted finishes, plus an extra depth, depending on the number of coats applied. Of the many types of varnish available, gloss marine varnish offers the most protection. When matured and wet-sanded it has a smooth surface that withstands heat very well. Marine, satin and flat varnishes are also hardy finishes, as are the old-fashioned resin-based varnishes which can be polished with rottenstone and oil after wet-sanding to give a soft satin sheen.

Although most varnishes tend to yellow slightly, some can be deliberately tinted to correct this. Yellowing is acceptable over most colours except white and pale pastels, while a little umber mixed in varnish to be applied over a red antiquing glaze gives an excellent result. Similarly, green pigment in varnish on a pale green ground gives a striking effect.

Constantly used surfaces which require a great deal of protection can be varnished in a number of ways, depending on the desired appearance.

All varnishes, particularly high gloss, should be left to mature for a given time. Heavy objects should not be allowed to come into contact with newly-varnished pieces for at least six to eight weeks as they may leave damaging marks. The following recipes should be chosen according to the finish required.

HIGH GLOSS FINISH

For a high gloss finish, apply six coats of high gloss varnish (see instructions below) and leave to mature for two to four weeks. Wet-sand (see below) and apply two or three coats of thinned down varnish over the next two or three days.

SATIN FINISH WITH HIGH GLOSS PROTECTION

Apply six coats of high gloss varnish and leave to mature for two to four weeks. Wet-sand, then polish with a car-cutting compound.

DULL FINISH WITH HIGH GLOSS PROTECTION

Apply six coats of high gloss varnish and leave to mature for two to four weeks. Wet-sand and apply two to three coats of flat varnish over the next two or three days. Although the finish will be dull, it will offer the same protection as high gloss varnish.

PROTECTIVE FINISH WITH WAXED SURFACE

Apply four coats of high gloss varnish and leave to mature for two to four weeks. Wet-sand, polish with car-cutting compound and wax with *carnauba* wax.

REMOVING DUST WITH VARNISH

One of the lesser known functions performed by varnish is to remove the dust that can appear in antiquing finishes. The dust comes from the atmosphere and from the tools used. Varnish, used correctly, can remove this dust.

Method: Apply two coats of gloss varnish to the piece. Any surface dust usually protrudes through the varnish. Once the second coat has dried for twenty-four hours, wet-sand to remove the dust. Be careful not to break through the varnish and damage the antiquing finish. After this process you may wish to add further coats of varnish, or polish with car-cutting compound then wax. It is possible to wet-sand some finishes before varnishing but take great care and use a fine paper such as 1200 wet and dry.

PERFECT VARNISHING

Perfect varnishing takes much time and practice and is difficult to master. Do not expect to become an expert overnight. The working area should be well-lit, dust-free and preferably not carpeted. A bathroom, with the bath and basin filled with water to pull dust out of the air provides a good workplace.

If possible, set up a varnish booth. When varnishing a large object such as a table, hang a 'tent' of damp sheets over and around the table so that dust cannot fall into the varnish finish. When working on small objects, make a canopy out of a large carton. Cut pieces of cotton to fit the sides, top and bottom of the inside of a box, as if it were completely lined, and use an additional piece as a 'tent flap' for the opening. (These pieces of cotton should be wrung out in water and then attached to the sides of the carton.) Before you place the article to be varnished inside the carton, spray the interior with water or mineral turpentine to pull the remaining dust away. Do not place the piece in the carton until you see the spray has settled on the bottom. Place upturned tins on the base of the box to hold the piece. As soon as the spray has settled, place the object in the box, wipe with a tack cloth and start varnishing. When the varnishing is completed pull the damp flap carefully across the front to prevent dust entering the box and falling into the varnish finish.

The atmosphere in which you varnish should be warm (25°C). If the weather is extremely cold and the varnish thickens, then warm the varnish in a container of boiling water.

Warning: Do not put the container of boiling water and varnish near direct heat as varnish is highly flammable.

Materials:

- **Cotton cloth**
- **Oxhair brush, good nylon brush or foam varnish pad**
- **Steel wool or 3M pad for abrading the next day**
- **Tack cloth**

Method: The conditions and technique are the same for either gloss, satin or flat varnish. The piece to be varnished should be wiped with the tack cloth immediately before varnishing. Dip the brush into the can of varnish to about 12 mm up the hairs. Do not overload. Place the brush in the centre of the area to be varnished and quickly pull it backwards and forwards, one stroke backwards, one stroke forwards and then one more stroke over the entire length to even out the preceding strokes. The next application should join up with this stroke. If it does not and skips are left, do not try to correct them at a later stage as the varnish will be setting up. The next coat will cover these skips. Watch for drips at the edges of the piece. Stop these with an index finger.

The application of the first coat of varnish over a painted finish is fairly simple, as the antiquing finish is quite absorbent and it soaks up the varnish. However, it becomes more difficult to apply

1. Hang wet cotton sheets over shelves. Spray the atmosphere inside with mineral turpentine or water to eradicate dust particles. 2. As soon as the dust settles place the object on the shelf, wipe with a tack cloth and varnish. 3. Slowly drop the sheet over the front of the shelves so that the object beneath is surrounded by damp cloth. Leave to dry for twenty-four hours.

subsequent coats. Once the surface of varnish starts to build up it becomes slick. Each coat becomes more difficult to keep smooth and free of the marks left by brush strokes.

Varnish does have a much longer drying time than paint. After the first coat of varnish is completed, leave the piece to dry for twenty-four hours. If the weather is wet or humid the varnish may take longer to dry. If it is not dry it will cling stickily to the piece of steel wool or 3M pad used for abrading.

Once the coat of varnish is dry, it must be abraded all over with steel wool or a 3M pad. Abrading is performed to take down any irregularities and to give the varnish a 'tooth' to hold the next coat. Do not abrade in the room where you intend to varnish. This should be done outside. When abrading is completed, wipe the piece with a cotton cloth and then with a tack cloth. Return the piece to the dust-free atmosphere and wipe again with the tack cloth immediately before applying the next coat of varnish. Continue this sequence for as many coats of varnish as desired, allowing twenty-four hours drying time between each coat.

> **Warning:** Do not use the dust-free work area to abrade as the shards of steel wool or 3M pad will remain in the atmosphere.

If the varnish used is high gloss, leave the piece to mature for two to four weeks before wet-sanding. This lapse of time is necessary otherwise the wet-sanding activity may break through a layer to reveal a jelly-like substance beneath. If this does occur, wait for the varnish to set up (usually overnight) and sand carefully to level the surface. Apply more varnish to cover the imperfection.

Satin and flat varnishes do not require this period of maturing. They also do not appear to pull so much dust out of the atmosphere — or require as stringent wet-sanding — as a high gloss. Satin and flat are not as tough as high gloss varnish however, and greater care must be taken when wet-sanding. High gloss varnish will mark if objects are left on its surface within the first eight weeks following completion. After that time it should not be susceptible to marking.

WET-SANDING VARNISH

To wet-sand a large area (or a piece which is large enough not to receive very careful inspection) use 400 or 600 wet and dry sandpaper. (400 is the coarser and 600 slightly finer.) When preparing a small object such as a tiny box which is to have the appearance of, say, Japanese lacquer, use 1200 wet and dry sandpaper. Having dipped the paper into water, sand using a circular motion in a straight row and return to interlock an adjoining row. Ideally, only one layer of varnish should be removed. When an all-over even dullness appears, wash under running water to remove any traces of scum. If the piece is too big for this, use plenty of clean water and cotton cloths and dry off with a soft piece of cotton towelling.

This wet-sanding step removes any brush strokes, dust and particles that may have fallen into the antiquing finish and the varnish. Once completed, the surface should feel absolutely smooth.

For a final high gloss finish apply two to three thinned down coats of varnish on consecutive days. The composition of this varnish is seven parts of high gloss varnish to three parts mineral turpentine. A dust-free working environment is essential and drying time between each coat is twenty-four hours.

COMPOUNDING

For a satin finish, rub car-cutting compound into the finish with a soft flannel after the wet-sanding process. When it is completely absorbed buff off with another clean flannel. This satin finish may require a number of applications. Make sure all the compound is buffed off before repeating the application.

WAX

Wax adds sheen and highlights to any surface. Wet-sanded high gloss varnish, compounded first with car cutting compound, makes a good base for wax.

Take a clean flannel cloth, load a tiny amount of wax and polish into the surface vigorously. When the whole area has been covered and the wax absorbed, buff off with another clean flannel. It is imperative that the first waxing has been absorbed and polished off, especially if a second waxing is required.

When another coat of wax is applied over the top of improperly buffed wax, dull patches will appear. This can be corrected by removing the entire waxed surface with methylated spirits. The compounding surface will also disappear and the entire process will have to be repeated.

For a satin varnish-and-waxed finish, apply two coats of satin varnish. Abrade each coat with steel wool, wipe with a clean cloth and tack cloth, then apply wax. For a flat varnish-and-waxed finish, substitute flat for satin varnish. It is an excellent finish for infrequently used furniture.

"LACQUER" FINISH

To create a superb high gloss finish apply ten or twenty-five to fifty coats of high gloss varnish following the above method of application and wet-sanding every ten coats. When the final coat has been wet-sanded apply two thinned down coats of varnish on consecutive days (seven parts high gloss varnish to three parts mineral turpentine).

CHECKLIST

1. Make sure the area in which you intend to varnish is dust-free.
2. Create a varnish booth or area with damp cotton cloths.
3. Spray the atmosphere with water or mineral turpentine.
4. Just before varnishing wipe off the piece with a tack cloth.
5. Carefully apply the varnish.
6. After twenty-four hours remove the piece from the varnishing area, take outside and abrade with steel wool or a 3M pad.
7. If there are any sags, abrade the edges to remove some of the ridges. Although these ridges may appear through each coat of varnish they should eventually be removed by wet-sanding.
8. Wipe with a clean cotton cloth.
9. Wipe with a tack cloth.
10. Spray atmosphere in varnish booth with water or mineral turpentine. Allow to settle before replacing object.
11. Return piece to varnish booth.
12. Wipe with a tack cloth.
13. Varnish.
14. Continue in this fashion until you have applied as many coats of varnish as you wish.

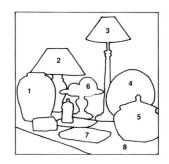

1. Copper leaf with verdigris overglaze and high gloss varnish. 2. An aniline dye glaze over Dutch metal and high gloss varnish. 3. A faux marble base and shade. 4. A gold leaf plate with hand painted design and high gloss varnish finish. 5. Crackle medium finish with gold leaf and aniline dyes and 25 coats of high gloss varnish. 6. Egg, left, black lacquered with silver and gold and oxidised Dutch metal leaf. 7. Black lacquer and gold leaf piece; faux tortoiseshell. 8. Red crackle medium and gold leaf trim.

6

GILDING

FOR CENTURIES ARTISANS have applied gold leaf to frames and furniture, performing the task in secret, with few allowed to observe the process. Now the technique of gilding is available to everyone. Although it is an intricate and demanding activity, the methods used in gilding are quite straightforward. It must however be performed perfectly for the leaf to retain its glow and clarity. The common metals are also used in gilding and chemicals can be applied to age the leaf so that a wealth of different finishes, including bronze, metallic and ancient pottery glazes, will appear at your fingertips.

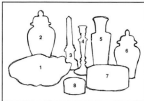

A selection of pieces with simple gilded finishes.
1. Ceramic shell in aluminium leaf with blue glaze. 2. Ceramic ginger jar with oxidised silver leaf over a simple glaze finish. 3. Ceramic obelisk finished in aged gold leaf. 4. Candlesticks with silver leaf and spatter finishes. 5. Ceramic vase with blue marble finish and oxidised silver leaf detail. 6. A good example of spatter finish. 7. Ceramic box with gold skewings over a blue glaze. 8. Handturned wooden box with gold leaf band.

GILDING IS THE LAYING of a leaf of either gold, silver, fake gold (known as 'Dutch metal' or 'schlagmetal'), copper or aluminium on a chosen surface. The leaf is fixed to the prepared surface with a mordant called size.

Preparation for gilding is of prime importance. It is absolutely essential that the surface to be gilded is free of imperfections. All leaf, including precious and common metals, will show up and exaggerate brush strokes, bad filling or poorly sanded areas.

The leaf itself is paper thin. Though once beaten by hand, today it is produced by very specialised machinery in most parts of the world except some regions of Asia where it is still possible to see leaf being beaten by hand. When held up to light, most leaf appears to be slightly transparent. The following types of leaf are commonly used for gilding.

GOLD LEAF
Normally 22 carat, the dimensions of gold leaf are approximately 37 mm x 37 mm, but the size varies depending upon the place of manufacture. All gold leaf is in books of twenty-five leaves. Each leaf is separated by rouge paper.

SILVER LEAF
Silver leaf bought in Western countries usually has a little alloy added. In Asia, however, silver leaf is almost always pure silver. Dimensions are usually 5 cm x 5 cm.

DUTCH METAL (SCHLAGMETAL)
Dutch metal, often referred to as schlagmetal, is composed of zinc and copper and makes an extremely useful substitute for gold. The sheets usually measure about 15 cm x 15 cm.

ALUMINIUM LEAF
This leaf is pure aluminium, usually available in the same form as Dutch metal. Sometimes it comes in packs the same size as silver — and in this case it can be easily confused with silver. To test if it is silver, place a drop of cupric nitrate (or any of the other chemicals for which recipes follow later in this chapter) on the leaf. If it curls and changes colour, it

is silver. If it shows no response to the chemical, it is aluminium. Alternatively, aluminium leaf can be purchased in large sheets measuring 25 cm x 25 cm which are useful for large areas.

COPPER LEAF
Pure copper leaf is available in the same form as Dutch metal.

> **Warning:** Do not allow fingers to come into contact with the leaf as it will disintegrate immediately. Even when a piece has been gilded, fingers must not come into contact with the leaf as they will leave an oxidised fingerprint. This occurs on silver, Dutch metal and copper leaf. On gold and aluminium leaf, contact with skin leaves an oily imprint which cannot be removed and any efforts to remove marks with mineral turpentine will remove the leaf.

TOOLS

- ✦ **White cotton gloves**
- ✦ **Vaseline**
- ✦ **Plant mister filled with mineral turpentine**

GILDER'S KNIFE
This is a long, sharp knife used for cutting gold and silver leaf. An extra-thin shoemaker's knife is a suitable substitute.

GILDER'S KLINKER
A klinker is a cushion on which gold and silver leaf are cut. It is made of a piece of board or heavy cardboard measuring approximately 15 cm x 10 cm. Cotton wadding or nylon batting approximately 2.5 cm thick is laid on the board and covered with a

piece of chamois which is then stapled to the underside of the board. The finished tool resembles a soft covered bed on which to lay gold and silver leaf for cutting. (See illustration.)

GILDER'S TIP
An essential tool, this is a brush of fine, long hairs set in cardboard. It is used for picking up silver and gold leaf and laying it onto the area to be gilded.

GILDER'S TAMPER OR MOP
This brush is used to tamp down the leaf once it has been laid on the surface.

SIZE
This is the mordant necessary to secure the leaf to the surface. Size is a varnish-based solution with additives to slow down and keep the drying time even. The most common size is called 'three-hour size': it can take up to three hours to dry and (depending upon how thinly it has been applied and the drying capacity of the weather) will then be ready for gilding. In good conditions this size can be ready for leaf within forty to sixty minutes.

A twelve-hour size is used when the piece being prepared is to be left to dry overnight. Because this size stays wet much longer than twelve hours, it is easier to work on large pieces as the size will not have dried out by the time the gilder is halfway through the job. However, when gilding with twelve-hour size the pieces should be dried for thirty-six hours before the leaf is distressed or patination is applied. Another disadvantage of using a twelve-hour size lies in the great amount of dust that may gather on the size during the long waiting period. In this case a tent of damp sheets should protect the piece.

1. Tools for gilding: tamper, knife, tip and klinker. 2. Make a klinker with cotton wadding, chamois and a stapler.
3. Smooth the wadding onto the board, cover with chamois, turn over and staple.

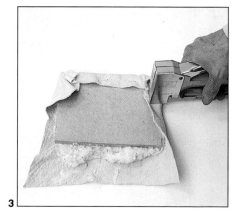

Ornamental eggs with gilded finishes: back, left to right, oxidised silver leaf, oxidised Dutch metal, oxidised silver leaf; centre, both eggs finished in black lacquer with gold leaf trims; foreground, black lacquer with gold and oxidised silver leaf.

BOLE

Bole is the name given to the paint used beneath leaf. The word means, literally, clay. Red clay was the original material used as the base for gold leaf. The reddish colour of the bole used today is most important as it throws up warmth through the leaf. It is an extremely acceptable colour, especially when breaking through the gold when the leaf is distressed. The term 'bole' is used for the japan paint applied to a piece to be gilded whether it is to be in gold, silver or the common metals.

Pale, grey-blue or black boles provide excellent bases for silver leaf. The colour of the bole to be used under silver is usually determined by the nature of the intended finish. Bole for aluminium is treated in the same way as silver and a deep green bole is excellent under copper leaf. The following recipes include the different bole types available for use with various metal leafs.

GOLD AND DUTCH METAL
- ✦ **30 mls Bulletin Red**
- ✦ **5 mls Yellow Ochre**
- ✦ **15 mls Chrome Orange**
- ✦ **5 mls Raw Umber**
- ✦ **1-2 mls White, if desired**

SILVER AND ALUMINIUM
- ✦ **30 mls White**
- ✦ **5 mls Standard Blue**
- ✦ **2.5 mls Chrome Orange**
- ✦ **2.5 mls Burnt Umber**

COPPER
- ✦ **20 mls Burnt Umber**
- ✦ **15 mls Standard Green**
- ✦ **2.5 mls Chrome Orange**

VERDIGRIS GLAZE
- ✦ **15 mls White**
- ✦ **15 mls Chrome Green**
- ✦ **2.5 mls Standard Blue**
- ✦ **Drop Bulletin Red**

Method: The instructions for preparation are exactly the same as those given in Chapter 2. On a flat surface apply three coats of bole allowing overnight or twenty-four hours drying time between each coat and sanding with 220 sandpaper. When the third coat is dry, wet-sand lightly with 600 wet and dry sandpaper. Be very careful that you do not break through to the surface beneath. Apply the fourth coat of paint and leave overnight, or for twenty-four hours. Sand with 220 sandpaper, wipe with a cotton cloth, wipe with a tack cloth and apply the fifth and final coat.

The following day carefully wet-sand with 600 wet and dry sandpaper. When the sludge has been washed off and the paint surface has dried, isolate with two coats of shellac, using a bob. Alternatively, isolate with two coats of water-based varnish. These two isolating coats are necessary when gilding as they help to ensure that there are no skips left for the size to penetrate, causing irregularities in drying time and blemishes in the final gilded surface.

When isolating for gilding the bob must be made of non-textured silk which has been washed to remove the dressing. Make at least two or three bobs, depending upon the size of the area to be isolated. When the first isolating coat is dry (about twenty minutes) apply the second. If using shellac, take some fine steel wool and carefully polish the whole piece after the second coat is dry. No ridges should remain from the shellac and the surface should be smooth. Be careful not to break open the shellac as this will result in irregular porous marks. Clean away the steel wool shards and prepare to size.

For surfaces with carving or existing ridges the preparation is slightly different. It is sometimes necessary to use a stiff brush to apply the bole to deeply carved areas. After the first coat abrade the surface lightly with steel wool, a good abrading medium on pre-gilded surfaces as the bole is invariably dark and can easily be further discoloured.

Depending upon the complexity of the carving, apply two or three coats of bole only. Intricately carved areas can be filled easily with paint. Do not let the bole drip or puddle and after the final coat is completed abrade lightly with steel wool. (It is impossible to wet-sand finely carved surfaces.)

After each application of steel wool use a small, hand-held vacuum to remove any remains. Be careful not to leave any residual shards as they can leave disastrous marks beneath a gilded surface. When the work area has been cleaned up, isolate the carved piece with two coats of either shellac or water-based varnish, using a stiff brush. At this point, do not abrade; the piece is now ready to be sized.

SIZING

Once size is poured from its original container it cannot be poured back so use in small quantities.

Dispense size into a very small container such as a lid. If the size is to be left out for some time, cover it with cling wrap to prevent evaporation. (If left for too long, it will become jelly-like and unusable.) The environment for sizing must be as dust-free as possible. All doors and windows should be closed and if possible, take a damp sheet and hang over a shelf. Spray the inside with mineral turpentine and place the article in that area on a stand of empty cans. Wipe with a tack cloth.

For a flat surface, use a silk bob made to fit the area to be sized. (Always have a contingency store of at least three bobs.) A stiff brush, No. 6 bright or 2.5 cm fitch, should be used on a carved surface. Pour a small amount of size into a lid, dip the bob in very lightly, pull across the top of the lid and then apply in an even straight stroke to the flat area. Reload and overlap with the next sweep. As the bob becomes loaded it will soak up more size and will need less frequent re-loading. Once the entire area is covered re-work the size to make sure there are no

skips in the application. When held to the light the sizing should appear even, slightly shiny and not too thickly applied. Leave to dry.

Be careful not to apply too much size to a carved surface. The use of a brush for application can cause a too-heavy application of size. The size goes a very long way and tiny quantities will suffice.

When the size has been sitting for about thirty to forty minutes (it is worth keeping a kitchen timer on

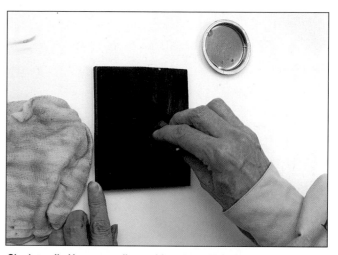

Size is applied in very small quantities with a silk bob.

Test the size to see if it is dry with a light tap of the knuckle.

67

hand), take a piece of clean cotton cloth and rub over the index knuckle to remove any natural oil and grime. Apply the knuckle to the size with the finger bent slightly and quickly pull away. If you feel a resistance to your knuckle or if a mark is left, then the size is still too wet. When you hear a sharp 'clack' and the knuckle feels no resistance the size is ready for the application of leaf.

Drying time is of absolute importance. If the size is too wet when the leaf is laid on, the size will soak through the leaf and absorb its brilliance, at the same time causing the leaf to take on a crumpled, crushed appearance. Although it is just possible to lay on common metal when the size is a trifle tacky, gold and/or silver leaf cannot be laid on anything but almost dry size.

A common fault with beginners is to imagine that the size has been applied evenly all over and, feeling some areas still to be slightly tacky, going ahead and applying the leaf. The leaf adheres in the damp areas but not in the dry areas. The application of size requires great skill and judgement which can rarely be perfected in one application.

GILDING WITH COMMON METALS

Your first gilding exercises should be carried out using common metals such as aluminium, copper or Dutch metal. Gilding with these metals does not require the use of a gilder's knife, tip or klinker. First put on white gloves. Take the book of metal, hold firmly and carefully cut off the spine. Now cut the book in half and then in half again. Place three-quarters of the metal in a box or envelope. Hold the pile of small cut squares of leaf in one hand and very gingerly with the thumbnail of the other hand, flick the very edges of the leaves which have been cut. This will force the leaves apart. As the cutting tends to mould the metal leaves together (and can cause them to break occasionally) this activity makes it easier to separate the leaves.

Take the top piece of rouge paper from the pile of leaves. Cover the top piece of leaf and gently slide it out of the pack between another sheet of rouge paper. Manipulate the pieces of rouge paper so that the piece of leaf is held between the two sheets of rouge paper with a small amount of the leaf dangling free at one end. Leaving about 7 mm to fall over the edges of the flat surface, lay the leaf flat on the surface and gently pull away the rouge paper. Using the tamper, gently make sure the leaf has adhered.

Take the next piece of leaf in the same fashion and overlap the first leaf and the surface edge about 7 mm. Continue in this fashion until the flat piece is covered. Gently tamp as each piece of leaf goes down, making sure the tamper does not come into contact with the size as this will redistribute size on top of the leaf. Small areas that have not been covered can be gilded using a quarter of the piece of metal already cut. Hold one or two of these pieces of leaf between two sheets of rouge paper and cut to size.

When the entire surface is covered, start working the tamper across the leaf in small areas at a time. Work the brush in a circular motion to help push the leaf down onto the size. This action will straighten out the leaf and remove any extra pieces left where each section has been joined. As you work see how the leaf flattens and becomes bright and shiny.

If the size has not been applied evenly, skips will appear where the leaf has not adhered because of dryness beneath. Conversely, the leaf will be wrinkled in patches where the size was too wet. In areas where there are skips it is sometimes possible to reactivate the size by blowing hot breath directly on it. Then quickly load the tamper with skewings (the residue of leaf created when tamping down) and tamp the skewing into the skip. Otherwise re-size the negative area alone very carefully and gild again when the size is at the correct stage of dryness.

Although it is possible to leave skips as they are, it is well worth starting with a perfectly gilded piece so that you will be able to dictate exactly where any distressing is to take place.

When the piece is thoroughly tamped down, the left-over skewings (the remaining metal pieces) may be kept in a jar for a small gilding job later. Common metal skewings tend to retain their wrinkles whereas gold and silver skewings do not and should always be kept for use at a later date. When the piece is completed it must be left to dry overnight and then wiped with soft silk. Now it is time to move on to gilding in silver and gold.

APPLYING ALUMINIUM LEAF

1. While the size is setting up, cut off the spine from the aluminium leaf. 2. Then cut the book into quarters. 3. Take a quarter of a leaf between two sheets of rouge paper and lay on board. Pull away rouge paper. 4. Tamp down leaf as you go. When the board is covered, tamp all over and clean off skewings, the small particles of excess leaf.

A decorative screen finished in silver leaf which has been slightly oxidised has a hand painted design. The edges of the screen (see detail above) have been finished using the bronze powder stencil method in Chapter 8.

APPLYING GOLD LEAF

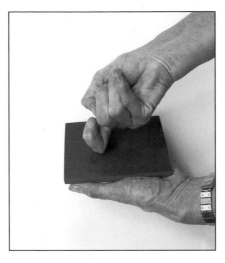
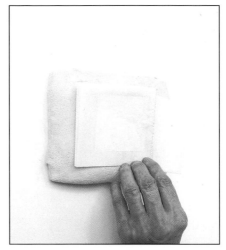

1. Apply size to the prepared surface using a silk bob. The application must be absolutely even. 2. Test for dryness. Apply a clean dry knuckle. A loud click on pulling the knuckle away means that the size is ready to receive gold leaf. 3. Lay a sheet of gold down onto the klinker. Slowly remove the book.

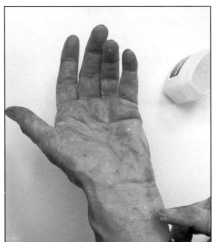
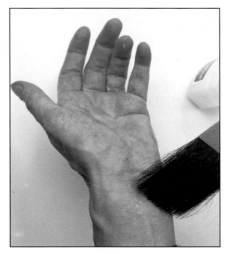

4. Gently cut gold into quarters with knife. 5. Place a small amount of vaseline on the wrist. 6. Rub tip lightly over vaseline.

7. Gently allow tip hairs to make contact with gold leaf and pick up the piece of gold leaf. 8. Slowly lower leaf onto board and gently pull the tip away. 9. Tamp each piece lightly as it is laid, then tamp the whole area when covered with leaf.

GILDING WITH SILVER AND GOLD

Materials:

- ◆ *Gilder's klinker*
- ◆ *Tip*
- ◆ *Gilder's knife*
- ◆ *Tamper*
- ◆ *Vaseline*
- ◆ *Talcum powder*

Gilders' knives are sometimes covered with an oil preservative. When used for the first time they should be carefully wiped on clean cotton. Before starting to gild sprinkle a little talcum powder on some clean paper and work the sides of the knife over this then shake off. Keep the talcum powder nearby so that if the knife begins to stick to the leaf at any time you can run it through the talcum again. (Do not allow the talcum near the sized surface.) If the knife seems to be a little blunt, pull it through a small knife sharpener. Some knives need sharpening even for the first application. Make sure there is no draught near your working space and do not cough or sneeze near the leaf as it will blow away.

Apply a tiny amount of vaseline to the inside of your wrist. Run the very ends of the hairs of the gilding tip lightly over the vaseline and put aside. Take the book of gold or silver leaf, turn back half the top sheet of rouge paper and turn the book over, laying the gold or silver leaf face down on the klinker. Gently pull away the book of leaf leaving the one leaf of precious metal on the klinker.

Take the gilder's knife and gently pull across the leaf to cut in half then at right angles to cut in quarters. Do not apply too much pressure as you may cut through the klinker. If the leaf is sticking to the knife run the knife through the talcum once more. Lift the tip and allow the very end of the hairs to come into contact with the edge of the leaf and lift again. The leaf will rise from the klinker attached to the tip. Slowly lower the leaf onto the surface of the practice board and allow it to lie flat (as with common metal). Gold and silver leaf is much lighter and more delicate than common metal leaf and therefore can be more difficult to handle initially. Continue to lay the leaf on the flat surface, tamping each leaf until the surface is completely covered. Tamp the entire area and place the skewings in a bottle. Where skips occur, tamp in the skewings. Now you will begin to appreciate the

Reproduction chair in dark green paint, gold leaf and two coats of flat varnish which has been steel-woolled and waxed.

Chess board finished in gold leaf with squares of oxidised Dutch metal. The containers are finished in black lacquer and silver and gold leaf. The ornamental quail is finished in black lacquer and distressed gold leaf.

superior qualities of silver and gold, particularly gold for its malleability, brilliance and colour.

Leave the surface to dry overnight and clean with a piece of silk or fine cotton the next day to remove any tiny pieces of leaf. Wear cotton gloves to do this. Gold cannot be oxidised but there are a number of ageing processes which can be applied to gold leaf (see Patination for Gilding).

GILDING RAISED AND CARVED SURFACES

Essentially, similar principles apply when gilding raised and carved surfaces. The only difference lies in the quantity of leaf used in application. One single leaf, when laid on a carved or raised surface, will break and cover only part of the area. Therefore lay on a number of sheets at a time so that when the bottom sheet breaks, the sheet above will fill in the broken area. Two sheets applied together are normally suitable unless the piece is very heavily carved, in which case it may be necessary to lay on three or more sheets.

When gilding a carved piece with common metal, make sure that there are enough pieces of leaf between the rouge paper each time you lay on the leaf. When gilding with precious metal the tip will easily pick up more than one piece at a time. Use the tamper to push the leaf into the cracks and interstices, and then to clean away the skewings. As with all finishes, the only way to master the intricacies of this technique is through practice.

71

GILDING ON A RAISED SURFACE

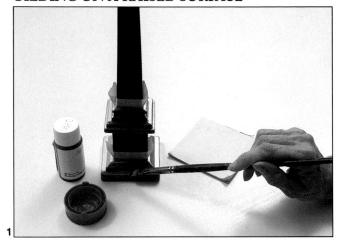

1. Size-raised areas with No. 6 bright. 2. Lift one sheet of gold with the tip and place on top of another sheet. Carry the two to the raised area. 3. Position the sheets of gold over the raised edges. 4. Press into the interstices with the tamper.

SKEWINGS

1. Gold or silver skewings can be applied at random over touch-dry size. 2. Tamp all over so that the gold or silver dust is distributed.

SKEWINGS

To create an attractive film of gold or silver dust over a piece, size the piece all over. The size must not be tacky and should be dry enough to run your hand over it. Brush the skewings over the piece, distributing the large and small pieces. After the application, pull a cloth soaked in mineral turpentine over the tamper to remove any size.

PATINATION FOR GILDING

Brand new gilding is extraordinarily bright and in most cases needs the subtle, soft look achieved by patination. Developed as recently as the eighteenth century, patination, the means of dulling and ageing gilding, is used to give a host of fascinating, rich effects and seemingly ancient finishes to a range of different gilded surfaces.

All leaf except gold and aluminium can be aged with chemical oxidants. Gold is impervious to oxidants but is successfully aged with paint, aniline dye or asphaltum. Aluminium is aged and dulled with paint glazes.

Oxidants, available from drug stores and pharmaceutical suppliers, are sensitive to light, heat and moisture. They should be kept in a cool, dry, dark place. With the exception of cupric nitrate, which can be stored, most of the chemicals used in the following recipes do not last long once they are made up. Start by making up a half, a quarter or even one-eighth of the given quantities.

> **Warning:** Do not allow skin to come into contact with oxidants. Do not inhale the fumes as they may cause injury.

Materials:

- ✦ *Small glass or plastic bowls and glass jars*
- ✦ *Plastic or glass medicine measures*
- ✦ *Plastic spoons or wooden chopsticks (for stirring)*
- ✦ *Cotton cloths*
- ✦ *Upholstery cotton wadding*
- ✦ *Plant mister*

The easiest way to measure the chemicals is to spoon the powder into a small medicine glass and add a small amount of the measured water. Stir to dissolve.

With some chemicals such as sodium sulphide and potassium sulphide this can take a little time. When the chemical is dissolved add the mixture to the remainder of the measured water in a jar. The water-based mixture can be poured from the jar into a glass or plastic bowl.

Most of the chemicals will last for two or three days or longer. However there is no hard and fast rule and sometimes a chemical can lose its efficacy overnight. It is wise to mix small quantities according to the size of the piece you intend to oxidise. In most cases only a small amount of oxidant is required.

CUPRIC NITRATE

Composition:

- ✦ *5 mls cupric nitrate*
- ✦ *2.5 mls ammonium chloride*
- ✦ *100 mls distilled water*

Method: Mix cupric nitrate and ammonium chloride in a medicine glass. Add a small amount of water and dissolve. Add the remainder of measured water and mix. This is known as Full Strength Cupric Nitrate. To make Half Strength Cupric Nitrate, which you will need for oxidising certain types of leaf, take one volume of full strength cupric nitrate and mix it with an equal quantity of water. Place this in a screw-top jar and label it Half Strength Cupric Nitrate.

SODIUM SULPHIDE

Composition:

- ✦ *5 mls sodium sulphide*
- ✦ *60 mls distilled water*

Method: Dissolve sodium sulphide in a small amount of the measured water and add to the remaining water. If the chemical will not dissolve, heat the water slightly and add it to the chemical. This will quicken the dissolving process.

BARIUM SULPHIDE

Composition:

- ✦ *5 mls barium sulphide*
- ✦ *400 mls distilled water*

Method: Mix barium sulphide with a small amount of the measured water to dissolve and add to the remaining water.

POTASSIUM SULPHIDE

Composition:

✦ **5 mls potassium sulphide**

✦ **60 mls distilled water**

Method: Mix potassium sulphide with a small amount of the measured water to dissolve and add to the remaining water.

APPLICATION OF OXIDANTS

There are numerous methods of applying oxidants to gilded surfaces. Upholstery cotton wadding gives lovely amorphous shapes when puddled onto a gilded surface. The cotton wadding should first be soaked in water and wrung out and then dipped into the oxidant. When wet it takes up the oxidant more readily. A plant mister is another invaluable tool to have on hand. A fine spray of oxidant creates a beautiful cloudy effect. Keep the spray bottle for oxidants only and wash it thoroughly every time it is used. Hessian (known as burlap in the USA), first wrung out in water and dipped into oxidant, gives a woven pattern effect when laid on the gilding.

When oxidising it is essential to keep a clean cotton cloth which has been wrung out in water close by. This cloth is used to lay down over the oxidant and neutralise it. Neutralising is performed to stop the action of the chemical. Gently place the wet cloth down onto the leaf and pat all over with the palm of your hand. Do not dab or rub as this action may damage the leaf.

There are some situations where neutralising is necessary immediately. However, in the majority of instances it is up to the gilder to decide when to neutralise the chemical. It should be remembered that oxidants, even when neutralised, or under varnish, continue to darken slightly.

Sometimes when oxidants are applied to leaf the immediate reaction looks frighteningly garish. Although this often occurs when sulphides are used on Dutch metal and copper leaf, the intensity of the effect usually disappears within twenty-four hours.

It is useful to be aware that varnish is impervious to oxidants. Therefore, when oxidising one area of leaf and not another, you may choose to varnish the area to be kept free of oxidising and continue to use the chemicals freely where desired.

Warning: Once you have completed oxidising the leaf, carefully run clean water over so that all the oxidant is removed.

This may not be possible to do without removing a little leaf in cases where you have used sodium sulphide and potassium sulphide which can damage the leaf.

Quite often when some oxidant remains, and varnish is applied over the leaf the varnish and oxidant can have a strange chemical reaction and the varnish can take days to dry.

PAINTS AND DYES

Gold, as it will not oxidise, can be aged with the alternative substances of aniline dyes, asphaltum or paint glaze. Distressing is another technique often used successfully on frames and raised surfaces which have been gilded in gold leaf.

To distress, take a piece of silk and dip lightly in mineral turpentine. Simply rub the area where you wish to remove the gold. The red of the bole will show through to give a luxuriant aged appearance. As years of exposure to the environment automatically cause the gold to wear off the high points of a frame — or any carved piece — it is practical, initially, to rub the gold from these areas.

If you are distressing a flat surface, pay special attention to creating a deliberately uneven pattern that will be aesthetically pleasing. This is one of the most difficult finishes and it takes a great deal of time and skill to be able to impart a true aged appearance to a contemporary piece, especially if it is flat. Once the gold leaf is distressed there are several more ways of adding to the effect. A spatter of aniline dye, the weight of which depends upon the desired subtlety, adds a rich glow. The dye can alternatively be stippled on, but in this case the gold leaf must first be isolated with a protective coat of flat varnish. Shellac is another possible isolating medium but since aniline dye is fixed with shellac it would be easy to pull off the shellac isolating coat when stippling. (Remember to use a silk bob for applying shellac as an isolating coat.)

A small diluted amount of asphaltum on gold leaf enriches the lustre and depth of the leaf enormously.

The chairs in a dining room setting are painted in green, detailed in gold leaf and finished with two coats of flat varnish which has been steel woolled and waxed.

From left gold leaf, spatter of aniline dye, top right, thinned asphaltum; bottom right, heavy application of asphaltum.

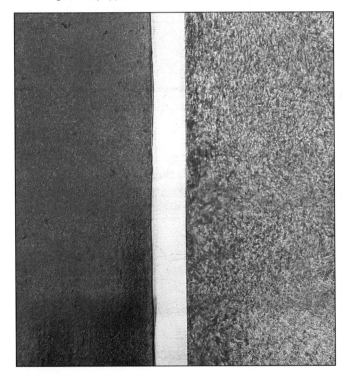

Pewter glaze, left, antiquing glaze, right. (Any colour may be used for this glaze.)

This may be applied either by painting on or by stippling positively or negatively. If stippling, isolate with shellac using a silk bob.

A translucent wash made up of casein paint (Pelikan Plaka is made of casein which means that it has a milk base), in a mixture of 90 per cent water and 10 per cent paint immediately dulls gold leaf to give

an aged look. If the piece is raised, this treatment is enhanced when followed by rottenstone which is loaded onto the carving, pounced in with a stiff brush and then emptied off.

On a not-so-heavily carved surface where you wish to see an inundation of rottenstone in the interstices, firstly wax lightly with carnauba (this is likely to remove some more of the gold). Buff off and then inundate the crevices and carving with rottenstone. The small residue of wax left behind will hold the rottenstone to the carving.

> **Warning:** Always wear a mask when applying rottenstone as it may cause injury if inhaled.

PEWTER
This finish works perfectly over aluminium leaf.

Composition:

- ✦ *20 mls White*
- ✦ *20 mls Black*
- ✦ *12 mls Raw Umber*
- ✦ *12 mls Burnt Sienna*
- ✦ *45 mls flat varnish*
- ✦ *50 mls mineral turpentine*

Method: Because of its content this glaze is known as a varnish glaze. It can be mixed in various proportions depending upon the amount of white, black or brown emphasis desired in the finish.

Firstly, isolate the aluminium with a coat of shellac, using a silk bob. Paint on the pewter glaze with an oxhair brush. Now stipple quickly with the stipple brush. The density of the pewter look can be increased as desired.

A variety of coloured glazes can also be applied to aluminium leaf. Using the recipe given above, mix whatever colour you desire and paint over the aluminium. A beautiful glow of silver will penetrate the coloured glaze.

TACHISTE
Tachiste, composed of casein paint, can be executed in any colour. It is particularly successful over silver and aluminium, though the aluminium shows through quite strongly. Generally, the tachiste finish should be applied in a misty, amorphous fashion. It does not need to be stippled on and therefore it is unnecessary to isolate the leaf with shellac.

Composition:

+ *10 mls casein paint (Pelikan Plaka)*
+ *150 mls water*

+ *One or two drops of liquid detergent (this acts as a binder and helps to hold the paint to the leaf)*

Method: Load an oxhair brush with the paint and lightly brush onto the leaf. Brush backwards and forwards until the piece is fully covered. Leave the piece and allow the water to evaporate from the paint. Weather conditions at the time of drying will determine the length of time for this evaporation to occur.

Tachiste can also be applied with cheesecloth. Load a piece of washed cheesecloth and pat lightly onto the metal until the desired effect is achieved. Sponges and pieces of damped chamois can be used in the same way as cheesecloth. When using chamois, paint the tachiste on with an oxhair brush and then roll a dampened chamois across the surface.

Tachiste is always left so that the water evaporates from the paint. The remaining finish resembles a fragile gossamer-like encrustation of colour. At this stage, the finish is extremely delicate and must be protected with either a coat of shellac applied with an oxhair brush, or a coat of varnish. Be careful when applying varnish. It should be gingerly applied so as not to disturb the tachiste. It should be thinned down to one part varnish and three parts mineral turpentine and even then it may pull off the tachiste. After the piece has been isolated a design may be imposed if desired and then the whole piece varnished in the usual fashion. (See Chapter 4.)

MOTHER-OF-PEARL

This finish is superimposed over a surface which has been gilded with aluminium leaf. The Pelikan Plaka paint used in the recipe below has a casein (milk) base which dries quickly and when used correctly gives a soft translucent effect.

Composition:

+ *Pelikan Plaka (casein paint) in Madder Red, Pale Blue and White*
+ *Cotton wadding*

Backgammon tray with exotic background of silver leaf. Oxidants have been applied to give the surface an aged look.

Elegant glass vases take on a pristine new look with, left, a mother-of-pearl finish and right, a pewter finish.

Method: Thin each colour with water so that it becomes quite translucent. The red thinned in this fashion will become pink. It is up to the gilder to decide whether or not it is necessary to isolate the leaf with shellac. When correctly applied this finish should not place too much stress on the leaf.

The colours are to be applied in the following order: red, blue and white. Puddle the paint on and allow each colour to set up slightly before applying the next. Do not leave drip marks. Leave some stained edges of each colour, that is, edges of more intense colour. Allow to dry overnight and apply varnish in satin or gloss.

ITALIAN PITTED SILVER

Italian pitted silver is always a favourite finish. To achieve this wonderful look of old dulled silver, puddle on half strength cupric nitrate. With the absolutely dry fingers of the hand not used to puddle on the acid, sprinkle on grains of salt. It is most important that the salt is not damp. It should fall off the fingers grain by grain so that the pitting will be very distinct. As soon as you see the grains starting to turn black in the silver, gently lay on a wet cloth to neutralise. To remove the salt, hold the piece under a tap. Do not attempt to wipe off the salt as you will damage the silver. If the piece is carved or contoured it will be necessary to apply the chemical carefully using a nylon brush.

Sodium sulphide gives silver a lovely pinkish tinge, but be very careful when applying this chemical as it will damage and neutralise after only thirty seconds. This type of silver finish can be distressed easily twenty-four hours after application.

Potassium sulphide gives a golden effect, while full strength cupric nitrate on silver, followed by an application of barium sulphide gives an immediate and very strong result.

Half-strength barium sulphide painted over silver results in a good finish. Asphaltum too, gives an interesting finish when painted over silver, particularly if the silver has been oxidised first with half strength cupric nitrate.

DUTCH METAL

Full strength cupric nitrate puddled over a Dutch metal surface and neutralised with a wet cloth within ten to thirty minutes creates a wonderful greenish bloom. If varnish is applied to preserve the metal the green will disappear. Therefore make up a verdigris colour (see colour recipe number 2) and dilute for translucency, about ten per cent paint to ninety per cent mineral turpentine. Paint and puddle onto the greenish-hued surface and leave to dry. On raised or contoured surfaces such as lamp bases, one quarter strength cupric nitrate can be brushed on with a nylon brush. Do not use cotton wadding on a contoured area, as the shape imparted by the wadding is unattractive. As soon as the metal reaches the desired colour, neutralise the piece.

Asphaltum can also be stippled on Dutch metal to give a wonderful effect. Before stippling, the surface must be isolated with shellac (using a bob). Also try spattering, dribbling or painting on asphaltum for different effects.

Full strength cupric nitrate left on a piece overnight eats right through to the bole. The next day take a piece of silk or fine cotton and wipe over the leaf. The leaf will come away where the chemical has eaten through and the rich red of the bole will appear.

Another excellent effect is achieved by puddling full strength cupric nitrate onto Dutch metal and then dripping potassium sulphide onto the finish.

Sodium sulphide on Dutch metal creates bronze, blue, then magenta tones. As soon as the magenta

SILVER

Variations on a silver theme can be developed using the following combinations. 1. 6 parts water; 1 part potassium sulphide. 2. 4 parts water; 1 part barium sulphide. 3. Aniline dye. 4. 1 part water; 1 part sodium sulphide. 5. Italian pitted silver. 6. Full strength barium. 7. Full strength potassium sulphide. 8. Full strength sodium sulphide. 9. Full strength cupric nitrate.

DUTCH METAL

Try these recipes for a combination of Dutch metal finishes. 1. Full strength cupric nitrate left on for ten minutes. 2. Asphaltum. 3. Full strength cupric nitrate sprinkled with salt and neutralised. 4. 1 part barium sulphide, 1 part water. 5. Full strength barium sulphide. 6. Full strength cupric nitrate left on overnight to eat through leaf. 7. Full strength potassium sulphide neutralised immediately. 8. Full strength sodium sulphide neutralised immediately. 9. 6 parts water; 1 part potassium sulphide.

COPPER

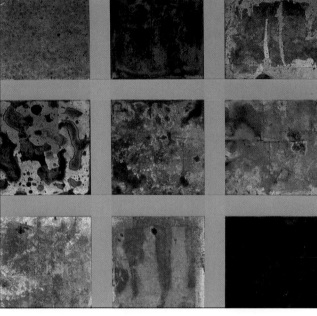

1	2	3
4	5	6
7	8	9

The following combinations give varying results over copper.
1. Asphaltum. 2. Full strength barium. 3. 1 part potassium sulphide; 6 parts water. 4. Full strength cupric nitrate. 5. Full strength sodium sulphide. 6. 2 parts water; 1 part sodium sulphide. 7. 4 parts barium sulphide; 1 part water. 8. Full strength barium sulphide. 9. Full strength potassium sulphide.

Oxidised gilding on a decorative plaster garden piece adds a look of richness and age.

is achieved (this may not take long), the surface of the piece should be neutralised with a wet cloth.

The same chemical may be left on for about twenty minutes, neutralised, then applied again for about five minutes. Neutralise once more, taking care not to damage the now-fragile leaf. Allow the leaf to remain untouched overnight and, if desired, distress the leaf a little further using a piece of soft silk or very fine, soft cotton.

A plant mister can be used to spray on the chemical. This gives a gentle, all-over inundation. Finally, try puddling full strength cupric nitrate onto Dutch metal with the right hand. Then with the left hand (so that it is absolutely dry) sprinkle over with salt then neutralise. Make sure fingers are dry when sprinkling the salt, otherwise it will not fall onto the metal in individual grains, but in large damp blobs. To remove salt the piece must be held beneath a tap. (Do not try to wipe the salt off with a cloth as it will drag and the metal will be damaged.) This finish is a version of Italian pitted silver (see above).

Barium sulphide can also be used successfully on Dutch metal followed with the same application of salt, as above.

COPPER

Because this metal reacts very quickly to chemicals, oxidising it can result in very harsh effects. One of the most satisfactory finishes is achieved using half strength cupric nitrate, neutralising and then applying a thin paint wash of verdigris green to create a realistic aged appearance.

Full strength cupric nitrate gives a slightly harsher oxidised effect and should therefore be used for a stronger looking final finish.

Copper leaf gilded onto red bole and then oxidised with potassium sulphide gives a lovely finish. The acid eats through to reveal attractive splotches of red bole all over the piece.

Try also one-quarter strength barium painted on copper leaf. Neutralise and paint on the leaf again. Neutralise and paint on the leaf a third time. Neutralise once more.

One-quarter strength sodium sulphide left on copper leaf for five minutes and neutralised also gives a good oxidised finish.

GILDING INLAY

The final appearance achieved using the following method is one of an inlay of precious or common metal leaf. To illustrate this technique I have inlaid a simple stencil design into a Dutch metal board. All types of leaf — copper, aluminium, silver and gold — can be used for this technique. Follow this example and then try out different methods for yourself.

The gilded board should be isolated first with shellac using a silk bob. (Varnish can be used as the isolating coat but it must be left to dry for twenty-four hours.) Using artists' tracing paper, cut a template to fit the sample board. Attach the template to the sample board with masking tape. Make sure the masking tape does not come into contact with the leaf as it will pull it off and ruin the leaf, even if it has been isolated. If you ever need to put masking tape across leaf, make a bridge of paper over the leaf and then run the masking tape over the top of the paper.

Using artists' transfer paper, trace the entire design onto the leaf. When this is completed, run your finger over the chalk lines left by the paper to remove any excess.

Pour a tiny amount of size into a bottle top. Begin to size the design, using Number 03 and Number 000 sable brushes to apply to the size. It is impossible to gild more than one leaf at a time. So you simply have to resize for the next leaf after the first inlay is completed. It is important to include the chalk line, and to apply the size evenly. There should be no evidence of skips or brush strokes in the size.

Warning: This is one of the most difficult feats performed in gilding and is often disappointing. Beginners usually lay the size in lightly around the edges and more thickly in the centre of the surface, precipitating uneven drying. If leaf is laid on in this fashion, the size has usually dried at the edges and the finished object is left very raggy.

When the size has been laid on the first area take a tiny amount of talcum powder in a lid and, with a Number 3 or Number 6 sable, carefully dust around the negative space. Make sure the space surrounding the area to be gilded is covered. The reason for this is to stop the leaf sticking anywhere but to the area to be gilded. If leaf glues itself down on another gilded background area it is difficult to clean away all the vestiges. Talcum powder protects the gilded background while also keeping it clean.

When the size is dry enough carefully apply the leaf which has been cut approximately to fit the area to be gilded. Tamp down and wipe away the excess leaf. Gingerly wipe the tack cloth over the next area to be gilded (not the newly gilded areas as the leaf will be pulled off). Make sure all talcum is removed from the area to be sized. Size for the next leaf following the above instructions. Continue in this fashion until the whole design is gilded. The next day the different applications of leaf can be oxidised and aged as desired.

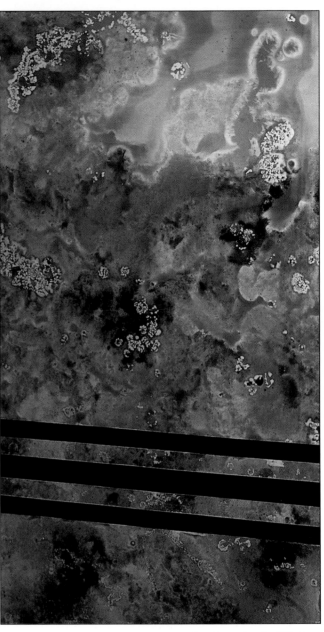

Black lacquered screen finished in oxidised Dutch metal and gold leaf.

7

JAPANESE LACQUER

The finishes illustrated in this chapter can be successfully performed on almost any decorative piece. Here, a lampshade finished in negoro nuri offsets a number of pieces also in negoro nuri, eggshell inlay and raising compound.

THE SUBSTANCE from which true Japanese lacquer is created is highly toxic and only available in certain Asian countries. This chapter gives the home worker the opportunity to use Western materials to create lacquered finishes which are very similar to the original Eastern finishes. While the finishes are extremely refined and require a great deal of time and patience to master, the results can be quite extraordinary. In particular, cherry bark, raising compound and eggshell inlay demand considerable concentration and expertise, but the depth and beauty evident in the final finishes is well worth the effort.

Ornamental goats finished in negoro nuri with oxidised Dutch metal detail on horns, hoofs and beards.

TRUE JAPANESE LACQUER is called *Urushi* and made from the sap of the tree *Rhus verniciflua*. Sap is tapped from this tree and after much refining, it becomes the lustrous finish known as Japanese, or Chinese lacquer. Other countries in Asia produce their own forms of lacquer, each from various trees in the one family.

Curiously, the word lacquer stems from the inability of sixteenth and seventeenth century Europeans to differentiate between *lac,* the substance used on objects made in India, and the medium applied by the Japanese and Chinese on their extremely sophisticated pieces. (*Lac* comes from the excreta of insects and forms the basis of modern-day shellac.)

All of the lacquer techniques described in this chapter are westernised versions of Japanese lacquer. Although they bear Japanese sounding names and produce a variety of Oriental finishes, they have been created using purely Western materials.

NEGORO NURI

This is one of the simplest and most popular finishes. Devised by the monks of the Negoro-dera monastery in Japan during the fourteenth century, it was used to decorate plates and dishes which were to hold and display food. Traditionally, the colours used for this finish are black and red. Black is used as the base colour, red is painted over and with some wear the black shows through. The traditional red colour was a dull, orange-red but Western taste seems to prefer something brighter. Other colours used for this finish are yellow and green.

The final sheen for this finish can be achieved by applying many layers of high gloss varnish, wet-sanding and applying two further thinned down coats of high gloss in an absolutely dust-free atmosphere.

(See section on varnishing in Chapter 4.) Alternatively, the surface can be burnished with steel wool for many hours followed by a number of applications of wax. The decision will vary with each piece, depending on the final look you wish to achieve.

Meticulous preparation is absolutely essential. Each piece must be filled, sanded and sealed with exceptional care before the varnish is applied, otherwise every flaw will show through. Preparation is the same as for gilding. Paint on three coats of flat black oil-based enamel paint with the usual sanding between each coat. Wet-sand the third coat and paint on two further coats of flat black enamel paint (leaving each to dry for twenty-four hours). Wet-sand the fifth coat gently until the paint surface appears absolutely flawless. Remember that if the piece is carved it should be steel-woolled between each coat. Wet-sanding is not carried out but the steel wool activity is a little more difficult and takes longer.

The piece must be isolated with two coats of shellac, and then steel-woolled until a mirror-like sheen appears. (If the surface is flat, isolate using a silk bob. If it is carved, use a brush. On surfaces with intricate carving, apply just one coat of shellac and abrade with steel wool as best as possible.) After cleaning up the work area and wiping all steel wool

For a perfect negoro nuri finish, bring the black surface to a mirror finish, then paint on one or two coats of colour. The top one must be opaque.

Before and after: a simple tray takes on new life with a negoro nuri finish.

shards from the surface, rub it over with the tack cloth. (See Chapter 2.)

Apply one coat of the desired colour. The paint should be as smooth as possible. If paint ridges appear on the surface, thin the paint. Allow to dry overnight and apply a second coat. It is possible to apply two coats in the one day if there is time for drying between the first and second coat. The following day the piece will be ready to be distressed.

Before distressing, examine the object closely and determine where the most wear would have occurred. The piece should look as if it has weathered years of use. It is vital that the antiquing should appear realistic rather than too distressed.

For this activity use 400 wet and dry sandpaper and water. Wet-sand the whole piece in a circular motion and then gradually start to wear away the coloured paint, allowing some areas to look more worn than others. This aged look should taper off so that the black is seen as little more than a shadow beneath the colour. Keep wiping with a damp cloth in order to see the finish you are creating.

If the piece is over-distressed simply apply another coat or two of colour and start again the next day. When the distressing is completed, wash off and dry. This finish then takes two overglazes: aniline dye and paint. If gilding is to be applied, aniline dye should be applied first. The piece should then be gilded and the paint overglaze added.

Aniline dye imparts a look of use and age and is applied by spattering. It will be absorbed by the paint which should be quite porous at this stage. Be generous as some of the dye may fade quickly. If too much dye is applied and the piece appears too dark, wring out a piece of cotton in methylated spirits and lay over the dark area. The methylated spirits will reduce the intensity of colour. Once this is completed, leave for an hour before applying the final glaze. Alternatively, gild where desired and then apply the final glaze as follows:

Composition:

- *One part of colour used to paint the piece*
- *One part Burnt Umber*
- *Three parts flat varnish*
- *Three parts mineral turpentine*

Method: This glaze is applied as a positive stipple. Load the stipple brush carefully and shake off on clean paper. Perform a positive stipple over about three-quarters of the piece. Build up some darker areas to create depth. When this is completed leave to dry overnight. Apply two coats of flat varnish for protection, dry and gently steel wool the piece before waxing. Alternatively, apply as many coats as required of high gloss varnish.

CHERRY BARK

This finish is the result of Western attempts to emulate the bark used to make Japanese boxes and decorative objects. It takes time and can be somewhat tedious, although it needs to be performed quickly. Cherry Bark is best performed on small objects.

Background colour composition:

- *1 part White*
- *.25 part Yellow Ochre*
- *.25 part Mid-Yellow*

Cherry Bark glaze composition:

- *One drop Red Oxide*
- *Five parts Burnt Sienna*
- *One part Standard Blue*
- *Asphaltum glaze (see recipe in Chapter 5)*
- *One orange stick*
- *One stylus*
- *Cotton buds*
- *Oxhair brush*
- *Bronzing powder*
- *Palette knife*

Method: Apply five coats of the base colour in the normal fashion. Wet-sand and isolate with two coats of shellac, using a silk bob. Abrade shellac with a scouring pad. Remember that since the background is a pale colour, it is not possible to use steel wool. Wipe off with a cotton cloth and again with a tack cloth.

Apply the dark glaze. The consistency of this paint should be fairly thick and opaque as one coat only is applied. Make sure no brush strokes appear on the paint surface. Leave to dry for sixty to ninety minutes, depending on the weather conditions. To test dryness hold the piece up to the light to see that the paint surface has a matt finish.

Leave for another fifteen minutes, then take a sheet of 600 wet and dry sandpaper (slightly finer than 400) and wet-sand extremely lightly, using a circular motion to ensure that the surface is as smooth as possible. In some areas a slight hint of the background will show through. This finish is not the same as Negoro Nuri; only very few tiny areas of stress should be allowed to show.

Once the surface is absolutely smooth, take an orange stick and, using the blunt end, pull away the paint in tiny irregular patches. A stylus and a cotton bud may also be used for this process.

Use water in conjunction with each of these tools. Once enough paint has been pulled away to give the look of cherry bark, leave to dry for twenty-four hours and apply the asphaltum.

Asphaltum is translucent and difficult to apply evenly. Paint on with an oxhair brush (no brush strokes should show) and then allow to dry. The drying process may take three days or even longer. Test by placing a hand lightly on the surface. If there is any pull, give the asphaltum longer to dry.

When you are sure the asphaltum is dry take a very fine piece of steel wool and, using a circular motion, pull away areas where there are ridges in the asphaltum. Try to vary the depth of the asphaltum. The application of steel wool tends to melt the asphaltum and to move it around.

When you are satisfied with the appearance apply two coats of shellac with a silk bob. The reason for these isolating coats is that sometimes when varnish is applied, it can disturb the asphaltum.

The shellac will stop this. Now coat the piece

The deep and subtle cherry bark finish adds a distinctive look of use and wear to a brand new wooden box.

with gloss varnish and allow to set up for about thirty minutes.

It is almost impossible to perform the next step without someone to help as you are about to apply a coat of bronzing powder using a tsu tsu tube. To make this object, roll a piece of clean, soft cardboard into a tube then place over one end a piece of fine hosiery secured with a rubber band. This tube is used to disperse bronzing powder into the air. Lightly load the palette knife into the bronzing powder, taking up only about one eighth of a teaspoon. Empty the powder off the knife onto the uncovered end of the tube. Hold the tube to your mouth and blow lightly so that the powder moves from one end of the tube to the other and out through the piece of hosiery into the air. Your helper should be holding the piece and, as the bronzing powder is blown into the air, he or she should wave the piece through the cloud of powder. This action should be continued until the application is satisfactory. The powder should be dispersed all over the piece in minute individual particles which create a fine, subtle veil of colour.

When performing this activity alone, try holding the tsu tsu tube about 30 cm above the piece. Tap the tsu tsu tube very lightly with a palette knife to disperse the powder in the air and evenly on the piece. After this finish has dried for twenty-four hours, the final coats of varnish can be applied to the piece.

Warning: Bronze powder is made up of ground metal and may cause injury if inhaled. When using a tsu tsu tube be careful as it is possible inadvertently to inhale the powder.

NEGORO NURI

1. Wet – sand board to create areas of wear.
2. Spatter finish with aniline dye.

CHERRY BARK

1. The base has been prepared and the overglaze is applied.
2. When the overglaze has dried to a matt state (about 1-1½ hours) leave for another 15 minutes. Then lightly wet sand with 600 wet and dry sandpaper.
3. With an orange stick or sharp wooden object pull away paint in tiny irregular patches. 4. The next day apply asphaltum glaze. Dry for three days or longer.
5. Gently steel wool the surface to give the finish high and low spots of colour. 6. Using a bob, apply two coats of shellac, then paint on one coat of gloss varnish. Allow to set up for about 30 minutes. Load the tsu tsu tube and either blow bronze powder onto the board or gently tap it out of the tube.

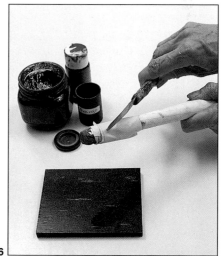

87

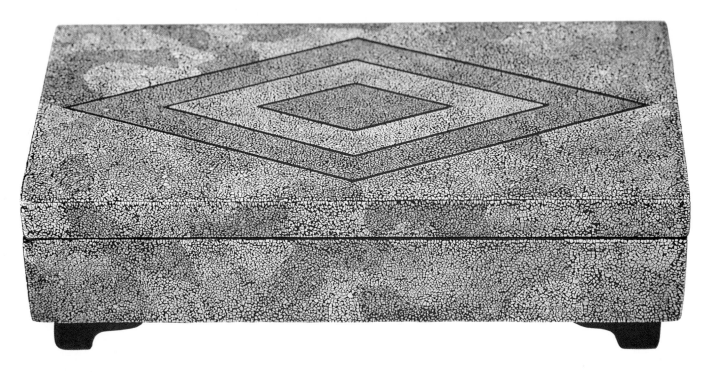

Fine pieces of eggshell inlaid onto the surface of a box give an unusual all-over pattern.

EGGSHELL INLAY

This is another time-consuming finish but one which is magnificent and rewarding when completed. It is becoming increasingly difficult to find contemporary pieces with this finish in Japan. Although eggshell inlay is performed in parts of the north of Thailand, the quality of the work is not as fine as that of the Japanese.

Materials:

- ✦ *Flat oil-based enamel or japan paint for base coats*
- ✦ *Ceramicist's pick*
- ✦ *Water-based glue*
- ✦ *Wax paper*
- ✦ *X-acto knife*
- ✦ *Number 3 sable brush*
- ✦ *Meat tenderiser*
- ✦ *Eggshells*

Method: As preparation of the eggshell requires one week, it is worth preparing a large quantity which will always be on hand when you need to prepare a piece of eggshell inlay. Some people keep boxes of eggshells for years.

Traditionally white eggshells are used, but brown shells will work successfully in conjunction with white. Although quail eggs have lovely speckled markings these tend to disappear during the treatment and the eggshells turn white. They do, however, give a beautifully fine inlay, despite being a little more difficult to use than hens' eggs.

Eggshells contain two membranes both of which must be removed, otherwise the eggshell which is laid down may fall off the finish when the membrane dries and the shell will lift away from it.

Having decided upon the quantity of eggshells to process, place them in a saucepan, cover with water and add two or three teaspoonsful of meat tenderiser. Simmer for two to three hours. (This same operation may be accomplished using a microwave oven.) Strain the water from the eggs and start to remove the membranes. The first membrane, discoloured by the meat tenderiser, will come away quite easily. It is the second membrane that can be tricky and requires considerable effort to remove. It is difficult to see and even more difficult to peel away. Keep running a fingernail over the inside of the shell to feel if it is free of membrane. If the membrane is still there the shell will feel slightly slimy; if not, it feels slightly gritty and offers some resistance to a fingernail.

Place the eggshells in a screw-top jar, cover with household bleach, and allow to sit for five days. After

EGGSHELL INLAY

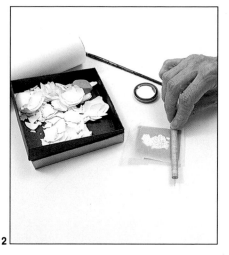

1. The prepared eggshells are broken into small pieces. The inside of the shell is lightly coated with water-based glue and laid, glue side down, on the board. 2. A piece of grease proof paper is placed on top of the eggshell and the handle of the ceramicist's pick is rolled over to fracture the shell into minute pieces. 3. With the pick, move each piece out slightly so that the final finish will appear to be an entire area of eggshell and not a mass of individually laid pieces. 4. Turn board over and trim edges with X-acto knife. 5. Grouting is pounced into the spaces and then smoothed over the top of the eggshell. 6. After 24 hours' drying, sand with 180 or 150 silicon carbide sandpaper. The eggshell will begin to appear. Continue sanding until all the grouting except that between the cracks has disappeared. 7. The finished board.

five days, remove from the jar and rinse the eggshells well to remove all the bleach. Place on a towel and dry well. The eggshells are now ready to be used. This is the stage where they can either be used immediately or put in a box and looked at and contemplated once a year!

Ideally, the piece to be inlaid should have a flat surface and a straight edge so the eggshell can be easily trimmed at the edge once the activity is finished. The entire surface is to be covered with eggshell. (See instructions for inlaying eggshell in a design at the end of this section.)

The surface of the piece should already have received three coats of flat oil-based enamel paint. It should then have been wet-sanded. Isolating is not executed as shellac would make the surface shiny, rendering it less able to hold the eggshell.

Keep on hand a small tin of water and a tiny amount of water-based glue (eg. Aquadhere in Australia or the UK; Sobo in the USA). Take a Number 3 sable brush, moisten in water and lightly load into the glue. Take an eggshell and break off a piece about the size of a small thumbnail. Moisten the curved inside of the shell with glue. It is most important that the moistening with glue is minimal. There should be enough glue to cause the eggshell to stick but not enough to seep up from beneath once the eggshell has been laid.

The application of the eggshell must be perfect. Starting in the centre of the piece to be inlaid, lay the eggshell, glue side down, on the surface. Take a piece of waxed paper, cut to fit the object being inlaid and place over the eggshell. Place the handle of the ceramicist's pick over the top of the paper and press so that the eggshell is fractured. Roll the pick back and forth across the fractured eggshell to make sure it is secured to the surface. Remove the wax paper and with the needle-like point of the pick, carefully start to move each piece out a little so that there is a tiny amount of negative space around each piece of eggshell. This will create space to hold the grouting.

When you are ready to lay down the second piece of eggshell, consider the whole piece and lay down the next piece of eggshell close to, but not jammed up against, the first. The finished piece should give the appearance of thousands of minute pieces of individually laid eggshell.

Make sure that you allow a little eggshell to protrude over the edges of the piece. Once the whole piece is covered, and before the glue has had time to set properly, turn the piece over and with an X-acto knife, trim off the irregular edges evenly. Allow the piece to dry for twenty-four hours then take some ready-mixed finishing cement, usually known as gyprock, or Victorboard F300 Finibond in Australia (in the USA it is called wallboard compound), and one or two teaspoons of a water-based paint such as Pelikan Plaka and mix the grouting. Take two teaspoons of finishing cement and mix in whatever colour you desire. Gyprock is putty-coloured and changes the tone of the colour that is mixed in.

Take a fitch brush and stipple the grouting compound all over the eggshell inlay, pushing into the cracks to make sure they are filled. When the cracks have been filled cover the eggshell surface with the compound and smooth with a palette knife.

Dry for twenty-four hours. The colour will have changed, often quite dramatically, but it will revert when the piece is varnished.

Now take 180 or 150 silicon carbide sandpaper and begin to sand the grouting, taking great care not to breathe in the dust. Eventually the eggshell will begin to appear. Continue to sand the surface until all the grouting except that between the cracks has disappeared. If the dust has discoloured the eggshell, take a piece of cloth dipped in a small amount of vinegar and very quickly wipe it over the eggshell.

Now apply a coat of non-yellowing spray. Incralac, a spray used to seal copper, does not yellow and is available at hardware stores. Spray this onto the piece (outdoors as the toxic fumes may cause injury).

To inlay a design of eggshell into an already-completed object, glue the eggshell to a piece of architect's linen. Cut out the design very carefully with sharp scissors and then glue down to the prepared surface. Alternatively, trace the design onto the piece with artists' transfer paper and lay on the eggshell as instructed above. Make sure that the pieces of eggshell are fitted evenly around the edge of the design. Otherwise the edges of the inlay will have to be trimmed with an X-acto knife and the knife may cut into the prepared surface and damage it. Be extremely careful when sanding off the grouting — do not damage the surrounding completed surface.

1

2

1. Make the compound following the recipe below, transfer a design onto a prepared board and using a sable brush, allow the compound to slide off the brush onto the design. Make sure you do not allow it to flow over the edges of the design. Clean back with an orange stick. When dry the raised areas may be gilded. 2. A completed example of raising compound.

A black lacquered vase with raising compound and silver leaf.

RAISING COMPOUND

This is an extremely useful finish which can be used on large or small surface areas. A good example is a vase where a design of, say flowers and butterflies, would be transferred. Each component would be raised and the raised area then gilded. Otherwise, take a tiny piece which has been covered with eggshell inlay and raise, say a tiny bug or flower on the lid or side of the box, and gild.

Before preparing the raising compound, coat an object with five coats of flat oil-based enamel paint. Wet-sand and isolate with shellac. Transfer a design onto the board with artists' transfer paper. Now make the compound and begin the raising.

Materials:

+ *65 gms ceramicists' whiting*
+ *30 mls gloss varnish*
+ *One teaspoon Red Oxide japan paint*
+ *Number 3 sable brush*
+ *Orange stick*
+ *Stylus*
+ *Ten drops cobalt dryer (this is toxic and may cause injury if inhaled)*

Method: Mix the varnish, paint and cobalt dryer in a tin and sift in the whiting. Dust in a little at a time to make sure there are no lumps and all the whiting is amalgamated. Dip the Number 3 sable brush lightly into the raising compound and allow the compound to flow off the brush onto the design.

The compound should not be brushed on; it should literally flow off the brush. Look out for potholes and any other irregularities as these will show up dramatically under gilding. While working use a stylus or orange stick to keep any compound away from the margin of your design.

When the design is completely covered, push back or wipe off any over-runs. If the raising is not suitable, wait until the next day to apply another layer. Do not correct mistakes on the same day.

If the compound is carefully mixed and applied it will last over a day or two while the process is completed. Put two or three layers of cling wrap over the mixture to make sure it remains airtight. If the compound has dried and thickened by the next day, discard it and start the process over again. Look closely though; you may find that a crust has formed on top and that underneath the compound is perfectly alright. Remove the crust, stir and use again.

Allow the raising compound twenty-four hours to dry and apply another layer if further areas need to be raised. When the compound has dried for the required period check closely all over and sand out any irregularities. Using a brush, seal with two coats of shellac. The piece can now be painted or gilded.

8

STENCILLING

THE GENTLE ART of decorative stencilling has been practised by artists and decorators in America, Japan and India for centuries. Stencilling, from the Latin *scintilla*, meaning, a spark, and French, *estenceler*, meaning, to sparkle, is the means whereby a pattern or series of patterns is continuously reproduced. Today this art is enjoying widespread revival with the delicate, simple patterns of the past reappearing on walls, floors, chests, trays, chairs and even paper and fabrics. The joy of stencilling is that it is so easy to perform. A child of five or a grandmother of eighty years can, with little effort and simple materials, create a charming pattern to transfer onto almost any surface.

Books of stencils are available from book and art supply shops, or you can design your own from oiled stencil paper, frosted acetate or oiled manilla folders. The most complex part of the activity is cutting the stencils: only a clean cut stencil makes a good design. Bronze powder stencilling, a slightly more advanced form of stencilling is also dealt with in this chapter. This involves the use of bronze powders instead of paints to give a fine, veiled effect.

The traditional stencilling part of this chapter was written by Hazel Tate. Kevin Tenney contributed the bronze powder stencilling section.

The charm of a country cottage! Random cornflower stencil pattern in ivory on blue ribbed boards with stencilled border stripes.

AMERICAN SETTLERS who were unable to furnish their houses with the rich fabrics, carpets and wall coverings of the old world used stencils and paint to imitate the patterns and colours. Many of the stencils were cut from tin or wood. Women eager to brighten their simple surroundings were the main practitioners of stencilling and the more wealthy hired the skills of itinerant stencillers. In the late eighteenth century, people such as Moses Eaton, Nathanial Parker and Erastus Gate became well known as travelling stencillers, who carried with them only a few tools, pigments, brushes and stencils. Examples of their work, seen in parts of America today, have been carefully preserved and are valuable as references for today's designers.

Just as the early American settlers took their designs from their surroundings (flowers, leaves, stars, birds, bells and the pineapple, a symbol of hospitality, were often used) so can we look to our environment for inspiration. There is virtually no object that cannot be adapted to take a stencil design.

Materials:

- ✦ *Masking tape*
- ✦ *Brushes (see below)*
- ✦ *Cutting board — a piece of plate glass, chipboard or plywood will suffice*
- ✦ *Tracing and carbon paper*
- ✦ *Straight edge*
- ✦ *Tape measure*
- ✦ *Saucers and old plates*
- ✦ *Rags and kitchen towel*
- ✦ *Hard, sharp pencil (for tracing)*
- ✦ *Artline 200 permanent pen (fine point for tracing on acetate)*

94

CUTTING KNIFE

The craft knives available in newsagents and paint stores are easy to use. Try when cutting not to grasp the knife too tightly as your fingers will soon tire and bruise. After a while you will master the technique of cutting, but persevere at first as your cut line may be shaky. When cutting oiled stencil board lean the knife blade slightly to the right (if right handed; to the left for left handed users) — this will give your cut edge a bevel and stop seepage of paint under the stencil.

OILED STENCIL BOARD

Recommended for single stencil designs. (That is, a stencil using only one colour.) This oiled opaque board is easy to cut but if used with acrylic paints the stencil will deteriorate as the board will absorb the water content in the paint. When used with japan paints or artists' oils the paint can be cleaned from the stencil after use with turpentine. If cleaned properly, the stencil can be re-used many times.

ACETATE SHEETING

An alternative stencil material, acetate is a transparent film which is easy to use and available from most art supply stores. The acetate is placed over the design and attached using masking tape. Using an artline permanent pen (fine point), you trace over all sections of the design and then cut the stencil with a craft knife. Always cut the stencil material to leave a one-inch margin around the design. This will help to avoid painting over the edge of the stencil board.

PAINT

When stencilling, it is essential for the paint to dry quickly. Matt finish japan paint in strong colours is the ideal stencil paint. The paint should always be creamy as watery paint seeps under the stencil.

When applying paint, take up a little on your brush and pounce out on a spare clean rag or paper before applying. Pouncing is a hammer-like movement that disperses the paint throughout the bristles. When an even speckling of paint appears on the paper the brush is ready for use. This must be repeated each time the brush is loaded. The brush is grasped like a pencil but held perpendicular to the work surface.

It is also essential to have on hand a large tin of flat oil-based white enamel paint in order to mix any colour you desire. Also keep handy black paint — either japan paint or oil-based enamel paint.

To begin with, the essential colours to have are Yellow Ochre, Chrome Green, Raw Umber, Bulletin Blue or Standard Blue, Bulletin Red, and in Windsor & Newton artists' oils, Rose Madder, Raw Umber, French Ultramarine, Lamp Black, Cadmium Deep Red and Yellow Ochre.

Hundreds of shades can be mixed from just these few colours and a white base. A little raw umber added will slightly grey any colour and give an aged appearance. If using japan paint, stir well because the medium and pigment tend to separate. When thinning use mineral turpentine. Stencil paint goes a long way so mix a little paint at a time, to a thin creamy consistency. However, if the mixture of colours is complicated, keep the stencil paint covered with cling wrap in an old tin or container and pour out only a little at a time onto a flat container. By taking paint up from a flat surface you will not collect too much in the brush and cause seepage.

Finally, before choosing a colour effect, test and play with several combinations. Using the colours, stencil a few proofs onto paper and place them *in situ* with masking tape (any large flat sheets of white paper will do). Leave them for a while and place the other colours which will be close by in the room around them. Walk in and out of the area a few times and you will soon know whether the effect is pleasing or not. Use the same experiment when choosing a background colour. It is very difficult when looking at small tins of paint or colour samples in decorator shops to imagine the overall effect a colour will give to a whole room, so try these early experiments.

BRUSHES

The best stencil brush is a soft, full cylindrical bristled brush. The bristles are approximately 2.5 cm long and end in a circular flat surface. These are available from most good artists' supply stores. Otherwise a selection of good bristle brushes from paint stores or newsagents will suffice. When using the brush pounce out well onto a clean cloth to make sure it is not loaded with too much paint. Never wash out a brush in turpentine while in use as the turpentine will stay in the bristles and run down causing bleeding under the stencil. If the bristles do need to be cleaned pour a little turpentine into a cloth and rub the brush into it to remove any caked paint.

Corner detail of a garden room floor shows how several different stencil designs can be interspersed to create a soft overall pattern. The two-colour stencil in cornflower blue and raspberry has been used on a subtle peach border. Right, the simple central floor pattern joins easily with the border. In order to ensure the permanence of the stencil design the flooring of heavy duty pineboard was sanded extensively, filled and given three coats of paint.

CHALKED STRING PLUMBLINE

A plumbline is essential when planning to apply straight lines on walls and floors. Two people are needed to snap a chalk line, unless it can be securely fastened or hooked onto the prepared surface. The device is held firmly by one person while the other pulls the chalk-coated string out. The string is pulled very taut and snapped or plucked in the middle, leaving a perfect, straight chalk line where it is needed. The string may then be rewound (shaken if necessary) and coated evenly for snapping the next time. Obviously when the stencilling is completed the chalk marks can be removed with a cloth.

PREPARING AND PLACING DESIGNS

For simple designs, using proofs or the eye alone is enough for arranging the stencils properly but for more complicated designs, measuring for decoration should be planned in advance.

To place designs on a surface, you may need to mark in guidelines. In the case of a running border, guidelines may only be needed on the surface which is to be stencilled. However, to centre a single design or to accurately place an all-over repeat design, guidelines should be marked on the stencil in ink with corresponding lines lightly drawn on the surface in pencil or chalk.

If total accuracy in the placement of the design is required, ie. the design is to be centred, find the centre of both tracing paper and stencil board by measuring the two opposite sides and mark with a pencil the middle of these two measurements. Draw a line across the paper between these two pencil marks and likewise on the remaining two sides. The point at which the two lines cross is the centre and should be marked with a cross. Follow this procedure on the stencil board and then on the piece to be stencilled, using chalk, which can be rubbed off later. When the two crosses are placed together the design will be centred. This method is particularly useful when decorating a tray, a table top or a chest of drawers.

A floor can be decorated with borders or a combination of borders and an all-over pattern. The border should be marked off first, using a chalk line.

Before starting to stencil a border, work out how many times the repeat will fit into the chosen area. Measure the width of a single repeat of the design. Measure the length of the surface to be stencilled and divide the design length into this. Mark a pencil or chalk guideline lengthwise on the surface to be painted and likewise make a registration on the stencil. After calculating the number of repeats take a ruler and mark where the repeats should be placed along the surface. Often the design will not quite fit into the space. If this happens, move and rearrange its position by expanding or reducing spaces between each repeat.

For marking truly vertical lines as a guide to accurate measurements on a wall, suspend a plumbline from the upper part of the wall so it hangs free of the floor or skirting board. A small nail in the wall will enable you to hang the line. Make only enough vertical plumblines to ensure the accuracy of the other measurements. The horizontal lines and the remaining vertical lines can be made with a ruler and a triangle, measuring from the plumblines and marking the lines lightly with a pencil.

The general care, repair and maintenance of stencils is important. A stencil takes quite a time to cut and is worth looking after. If cared for and stored properly it can be used again and again. To clean the stencil after it has been used, remove all masking tape, spread clean newspapers on the table and cover with several layers of paper towelling. Place the stencil on the towels and using a tissue or soft cloth moistened with turpentine, wipe with a firm motion. Do not rub — you may catch and tear the stencil. Clean both sides and store flat in an old envelope or folder. If a stencil tears, usually on one of the stencil bridges, cut a small piece of clear tape and stick either side of the tear. If necessary, re-cut the pattern where the tape intrudes.

MAKING A STENCIL

You will see from the illustrations on these pages that my stencil design is inspired by a rose pattern on some chintz fabric. In order to do this I roughly sketched out my version of the rose pattern, breaking down the design so that no two sections were touching. When drawing your own designs, the easiest way

MAKING A STENCIL

1. Using fabric or a picture as inspiration, make a sketch onto paper. By breaking up all sections of the drawing so that no two parts of it are touching, the design can be transferred easily onto stencil board to create a single stencil design. This is done using tracing paper, carbon paper and oiled stencil board and leaving a clear cutting line on the stencil board. 2. Cut each section of the design out using a cutting board and a sharp craft knife. Draw the knife towards you and cut down the right hand side of each pattern section, turning the stencil and returning along the uncut edge. 3. The stencil is now ready to use. Place it in position for painting and secure with masking tape. 4. Tip a small amount of paint into a wide, flat-bottomed container. Take a stencil brush and dip sparingly into paint. Pounce brush onto cloth to remove any surplus paint. Too much paint will cause bleeding and smudging. Gently stipple the brush over the stencil until the whole design is covered. 5. Lift the stencil carefully and move on to the next print.

Far left, a simple stencil design of a vase and flowers on a sponged background transfers to become a decorative fireboard, left.

to do this is to make your drawing as lifelike as possible. Do not worry about the breaks and when you are happy with your work, break down the design forming the bridges, these being the spaces between each section of the stencil design. If you did not form these bridges and sections you would be left with a large area of painting and no definition.

If the illustration, fabric, wallpaper or other source of your inspiration is more complicated you can simplify your drawing or even stylise it as in the Art Nouveau style.

Once the drawing is completed, the design must be transferred to the stencil material. In order to do this cut the stencil board, carbon paper and tracing paper, allowing a 2.5 cm margin on the stencil board around the edge of the design. Cut the tracing paper the same size as the stencil board. Place the sheet of tracing paper over the design and make a hinge at the top with masking tape. Trace carefully over the lines making sure the design is centred and that there is a 2.5 cm margin all around. Place the tracing paper over the stencil board and sandwich the carbon between the two, making sure the inky side faces down towards the stencil board. Hinge again at the top with masking tape. Using a hard pencil or old ball point which has dried up, trace over your design, occasionally lifting the tracing to check that you have completed all sections of the design.

When tracing is completed take away the tracing and carbon paper and remove the masking tape. Place the stencil on a cutting surface. Suitable cutting surfaces are hardwood, a piece of plate glass with the edges taped or a stack of old newspapers. The stencil is placed on the cutting surface and allowed to move freely. Take a stencil knife and hold as you would a pencil, trying not to grip too tightly. Try to lean the blade of the knife slightly to the right. This will give your cut edge a slight bevel which will help to stop paint seepage. When cutting, apply even pressure for the entire length of a line or curve. Frequent lifting of the knife blade will cause jagged and uneven edges which will affect your final print and cause ragged lines. Hold the stencil in place and with your non-cutting hand guide the stencil around any curves. Cut the smaller sections of the design first to avoid weakening the stencil. Keep the blade of the knife sharp at all times — snap off used blades to reveal new ones. Circles and small dots are impossible to cut with a knife. Use a leather punch which has various hole sizes, or knitting needles and ordinary large size needles will do. Then carefully clean up the hole using a piece of fine sandpaper.

At last the stencil is ready to print. Having carefully chosen your stencil position, use masking tape to hold the stencil in place. Then, remembering not to load the brush with too much paint and having pounced the brush out on clean cloth to gain an even speckled look, gently stipple all the open sections of the stencil until they are filled with colour. If your brush is not loaded with too much paint you should have an even print and be ready to move on to complete the next stencil in your pattern.

BRONZE POWDER STENCILLING

By far the simplest and fastest way of achieving an apparently gilded decoration is to apply bronze powders through a stencil onto varnish which is almost dry. This technique was used in Oriental decoration for many centuries and became extremely popular in the United States during the first half of the nineteenth century.

The emergence of a prosperous middle class created a demand for furniture decorated in the manner of Sheraton, Adam and the masters of the Regency and Empire styles. Pieces enriched by ormolu, brass and fine gilding soon gave way to the simplified method of stencilling which could be applied with speed and very little expense.

The most prolific American furniture manufacturer was Lambert Hitchcock, whose factory at Hitchcocksville in Connecticut produced chairs by the thousands. Paintwork, mainly in black but also dark green, red or brown, served as an ideal background for the brilliant powders; it also unified the variety of timbers which could be found in one piece of furniture. Other backgrounds were painted to simulate rosewood and mahogany, adding even greater richness, and occasionally the actual timbers were also patterned using stencil designs and paints.

During the first quarter of the nineteenth century, designs were created by carefully placing many single stencils and shading them elaborately to create depth in the designs. Later, pieces displayed a simpler one-piece stencil technique which was developed to cope with the increased demand, and by the eighteen-sixties standards had declined greatly.

Early work was executed with stencils of oil paper. These were later replaced by tracing cloth (also called architects' linen) which gave greater strength and durability combined with a degree of transparency which assisted in the placement of patterns. Although this is still the best medium it is becoming increasingly difficult to find and the modern equivalent which has replaced it in drawing offices is plastic tracing film. This makes an acceptable stencil.

When making a stencil, choose a translucent film with a glossy and dull side. The glossy side is placed down on the varnish while the dull side is a perfect surface on which to draw the design. The same technique applies to architects' linen, if you are fortunate enough to find it.

Pencil box, far right, is paint grained and stencilled using bronze powders and striped. Right, an old coal scuttle is easily restored with a decorative stencil design. The border and handle are in Dutch metal leaf pounced with asphaltum.

Classic reproduction Boston
rocking chair, left, is decorated
with smoke graining and
traditional bronze powder
stencils. Right, fine details add a
dainty touch to a sidetable
which has been painted, striped,
stencilled and marble painted
in naive marble.

BRONZE POWDER STENCILLING

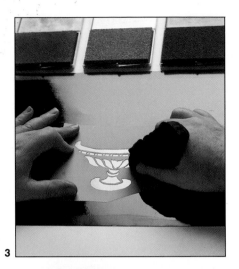

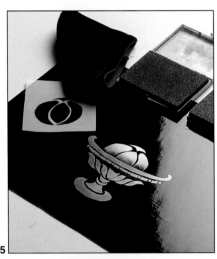

1. Trace the individual elements of your design onto stencil material. 2. Cut the stencil out on glass. 3. Once varnish has reached the right tack, position the stencil and apply the powder. 4. The first stencil is completed. 5. Position the second stencil, highlight and shade into bowl. 6. Shade the third and fourth stencils into position. 7. Shade the leaf stencil just over the edge. 8. Apply veining to the centre of the leaves. 9. Position small leaf fillers to balance the design and apply red fire powder over the fruits and the bowl. 10. Far right, see the completed design applied to a tray.

TRACING DESIGNS

Fruit and flowers overflowing from baskets and cornucopias were by far the most popular stencil themes during the early years of the nineteenth century. As cheerful and pretty symbols of abundance and hospitality, they appeared on thousands of chair backs. Classical motifs from the Greek and Egyptian styles also found their place, particularly in later one-piece work. Shells appeared on work produced in the seaport cities of Boston, Baltimore and New York. If you do not feel up to drawing your own there are many books of cut-and-use stencils available. Although these are designed for paints and the thickness of the card makes them unsuitable for bronze powder stencilling, the designs may be traced onto a finer stencil medium. Use these in their one-piece form or break them into separate elements to facilitate shading and the use of different colours.

The ideal baseboard is a sheet of glass, which later provides an excellent cutting surface. Tape down the original pattern, and tape the stencil material with the dull side up. Using a hard pencil (2H), an ink pen or a fineline marker, trace the design taking care to allow a generous margin all round — at least 5 cm — to protect the varnish from unwanted powder. Keep the lines as fine and accurate as possible to ensure a sharp stencil. Draw separate stencils for each element and trace in sections of the surrounding design to assist in registering the pattern.

CUTTING THE STENCIL

The powders are so fine they will creep under the stencil edge unless it is absolutely flat; therefore, glass serves as an ideal cutting base. This is particularly important when cutting linen. Choose the cutting tool which gives you the greatest comfort and control. Stencil knives, single-edge razor blades, artists' scalpels and fine, sharp scissors are all useful, as are the craft knives with snap-off blades. Whatever you choose must be sharp. Only a crisp, finely cut stencil will produce good finished work. Try to retain flowing curves as you cut, as any jagged edges will show up. Working with a knife, hold the blade still in position and turn the stencil as you cut. Always cut towards the area you are removing; cut away from points, not towards them as the slightest cut beyond your design will allow powder to seep through and

10

muddy your work. Very small circles can be cut with punches used in leather and craft work.

THE POWDERS

Bronze powders are available in a wide range of colours with shades of gold, silver and copper used in traditional patterns and pastel colours added for modern effects. Gold leaf powder is more expensive; however, its brilliance and permanency make it a worthwhile investment. Bronze powders will tarnish and darken slightly in time. However if an instant aged effect is desired they are often finished with an antiquing varnish.

A velour palette is the traditional utensil for storing and using the powders. Small mounds of powder are worked into the pile and lifted off for application. The velour is then carefully folded to hold the powders in position. An alternative is a small shallow box or tin. Use one for each colour with a pad of foam plastic fitted inside to hold the powder. Make sure the lid fits tightly.

You are now ready to stencil. But not on a box or tray just yet. First, practise by registering your patterns on black cardboard or heavy paper to which you have applied two coats of flat black enamel, then proceed as below.

Method: Apply a coat of gloss varnish over a well-prepared and sanded surface. Allow to stand until almost dry. As the weather and the varnish will vary, test for the right tack by lightly touching a clean knuckle to the varnish at ten-minute intervals. You

Tracing linen stencils must be cleaned regularly using lighter fluid.

the varnish, building it up little by little and burnishing heavily for highlights. Be sparing and be careful. Do not run over the outside edge of your stencil. Do not scatter powder by being too vigorous. Do not blow on it. Remember how fine the powder is and how easily it will settle on the varnish just where you do not want it. If the worst does happen do not attempt to clean up until the next day when the varnish is completely dry.

Be sure to keep the stencils clean. The shiny side can easily pick up surplus powder and deposit it again on the varnish. A cloth lightly dampened with lighter fluid is the best cleaning agent, and essential if you are using architects' linen.

After twenty-four hours, wash down with a damp cloth and then dry the piece thoroughly. If you need to clean up, a pencil eraser will work wonders, while larger areas can be treated with kitchen cream cleanser on a damp cloth. Re-touching with the background colour is also possible and later coats of varnish will conceal this.

> **Warning:** Failure to wash down the piece will mean the spreading of loose powder all over your work when you apply the first coat of protective varnish.

To finish, apply at least two coats of varnish which should then be rubbed down in the usual way. For an antique finish, mix spots of black and burnt umber artists' oil or japan paints into varnish and apply as many coats as you need to create the desired effect before finishing with clear varnish.

are ready to start when your knuckle comes away with a sharp click, leaving no impression. The usual time is about one hour. Resist the temptation to begin earlier; if the varnish is too wet the powder will drown and lose its brilliance. The powder should sit on the surface rather than be buried in the varnish.

Once the tack is right you will be able to work for quite a while. Even when varnish feels dry it will still accept the powder (sometimes where you do not want it). If, however, it does become too dry, wait until the next day, wash the piece down, re-varnish and continue the process. Lay the stencil in position on the varnish, shiny side down. Gently press the edges by laying a piece of waste stencil material over it.

The powder is applied by wrapping your forefinger in a material which will not leave an impression of weave. The best fabric is silk velvet but chamois or soft leather may also be used. Be sure to draw the material flat over the ball of your finger so that no creases occur.

Powder is applied by pressure on the ball, not the tip of your finger. Touch lightly into the powder, tap off any surplus onto a pad of paper beside you and then, beginning on a solid area of the stencil and using a circular motion, lightly work the powder over

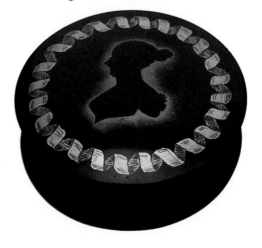

Black painted box, left, has silhouette in reverse stencilling with border of etched gold leaf curling ribbon. Right, shades of the orient in a tray with stencilled design and freehand bronzing on tortoiseshell background.

9 | MARBLING

Marbled walls, skirting
boards and a faux marble
column create an image of
bygone grandeur in a
formal city restaurant. The
marble finishes were
designed to complement
the colour scheme of the
restaurant and the
columns received extra
coats of varnish to set
them aside as decorative
features.

THE SUBLIME, FLUID FORMATIONS and myriad of colours evident in real marble have provided inspiration for painters for hundreds of years. Today the process of recreating the natural look of marble is still one of the most fascinating and challenging of painted finishes. To understand the diversity of the marbling techniques described in this chapter, it is worthwhile spending some time studying marble in as many different settings and environments as possible. Photographs from magazines and books often show exceptional pieces and lobbies or reception areas of public buildings often display good examples of real marble.

Books with examples of marbling by masters of the craft provide an invaluable source and an adjunct to learning the process. To sample the real thing, buy off-cuts of marble from stonemasons or vanity basin manufacturers. But be careful: owning a large number of heavy marble pieces can be a nuisance. They can be cumbersome objects to store. Try to keep just a few very special pieces.

THE FINISHES DESCRIBED in this chapter are simple and straightforward. To create these finishes successfully takes a great deal of patience, time and practice. When marbling, you must learn to think only in amorphous, drift-like shapes. Straight lines are no longer to exist. If you follow the directions given for each finish and study the step-by-step photographs you will master these finishes easily. For practising, have on hand several boards of white plastic-coated masonite measuring approximately 60 cm x 60 cm, or plain white off-cuts of laminex or another substance with a slick surface with enables you to wipe off finishes and start again. On furniture and small decorative objects follow normal preparation methods. (See Chapter 2.)

QUICK BLACK MARBLE

Materials:

+ *One part flat White oil-based enamel paint*
+ *One part scumbling medium*
+ *Nine parts mineral turpentine*
+ *Semi-gloss Black enamel paint*
+ *Sponge*
+ *Feather*
+ *Number 3 sable brush*
+ *Cotton T-shirt material*

Method: Take a sample board and paint with three thinned coats of semi-gloss black enamel. (If applying this finish to a piece of furniture, use flat black oil-based enamel paint which would then be wet-sanded and isolated.) Wring out the sponge in water. Load very lightly into the white glaze. Wring out carefully so that there is very little paint on the sponge and apply a few light drifts to the board. This application must be very pale, almost indiscernible. It will set up very quickly as it is made mostly of mineral turpentine. Take a piece of cotton T-shirting and dab and pat the drift, removing and blurring some of the paint.

Now take a feather and dip into white paint which has the consistency of thin cream. Take off any excess on butchers' paper and draw the feather across the face of the board in a large fluttery vein. If you find your application is a little too heavy take the T-shirt-

ing material again and dab the vein lightly here and there, allowing some of the black to show through. This vein should have some degree of translucency.

Take the Number 3 sable brush and lightly load into the mix used for the feather. Holding it between the thumb and index finger, pull across the board, turning and rolling as you go, creating fine, thin veins. There should always be an appearance of translucency in these veins. If the veins appear heavy rub lightly with a piece of T-shirting to remove some paint and allow the black to shine through.

With the very tip of the Number 3 sable, or if you prefer, with the Number 000 sable, pull a network of tiny, fine veins through the marble. For this finish to appear realistic it requires a number of coats of high gloss varnish.

MARBLE FOR TERRACOTTA POTS

This is a favourite finish which is quick and easy. Although devised for pots it can be used on almost any other object. Choose a pot which does not have many ridges or raised or carved decoration. This marble works best on a flat surface.

Materials:

+ *Flat water-based paint in Green, Black and White*
+ *Sponges*
+ *Feathers*

Method: Paint the pot all over with the quick-drying green flat paint. When the base coat is dry take the sponge which has been wrung out in water, load lightly into black paint and run drifts of black over the green. Allow some areas to be darker than others to give some depth to the application.

Now use a pale green paint with another sponge which has first been wrung out in water. Run drifts over the black. Do not apply all over — and not as densely as the black. The pot is now ready to be veined. Dip the feather into thinned white paint. Drag the edge of the feather diagonally along the pot from bottom to top. Position some veins on the edges of denser areas of the drifts at equal distances. It is better to have too few veins than too many. Leave overnight to dry and apply two coats or more of marine varnish for protection and waterproofing.

QUICK BLACK MARBLE

1. Prepare as usual with eggshell paint. Wring out sponge in water. Load lightly into white glaze and run drifts across the board. 2. Smudge drifts with soft cotton and remove all high contrasts. 3. Dip a feather into white paint which has the consistency of cream and apply veins. Use a No. 3 sable brush for smaller veins.

MARBLE FINISH FOR TERRACOTTA POTS

1. Wring out sponge in water and load into black water-based paint. The pot has already been painted with water-based green paint. Dry for one hour. 2. Run drifts of white water-based paint over the black (not too dense). 3. Apply veins with a feather and sable brushes.

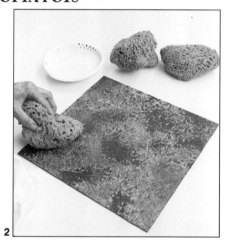
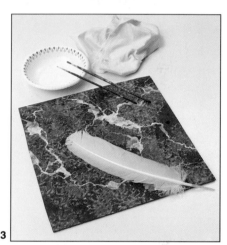

FOOLPROOF MARBLE

1. Paint on glaze and stipple to remove any brush strokes. Using crumpled tissue paper, fracture the paint to create drifts.
2. Fracture diagonally with concertinaed newspaper.
3. Apply veins with a feather and sable brushes.

Left, a charming old tin hat box received a naive marble finish in terracotta, accented in grey and white veins. Right, a soft marble finish in cream places subtle accent on both doorways.

Gloss varnished chest in quick black marble finish with silver leaf handles and bases.

Terracotta pots with green marble finish add a new dimension to the garden.

![box]

A box or casket has been given a foolproof marble finish with cream drifts applied with a feather.

FOOLPROOF MARBLE

This marble is best executed in high contrast colours and easily completed on a 60 cm x 60 cm board. A white background with colours such as burgundy, black, dark green or brick red creates a good finish.

Materials:

- *One part japan or flat oil-based enamel paint*
- *One part scumbling medium*
- *One part mineral turpentine*
- *Oxhair brush*
- *Stipple brush*
- *Feather*
- *Newspaper*
- *Tissue paper*
- *Number 3 sable brush*

Method: Have ready two or three pieces of broadsheet newspaper which have been folded, concertina style, diagonally across. Each fold should be about 2.5 cm. Fold also two or three sheets of tissue paper in the same way, and have on hand two or three lightly crumpled sheets of tissue paper.

Paint the glaze on and stipple to remove the brush strokes. Holding the concertinaed newspaper in both hands, pounce diagonally across the board to create large fractured marks. With a piece of crumpled tissue paper, start to fracture the paint in a drifting motion. Now take a piece of concertinaed tissue paper and run tinier, less graphic fractures across the board. If desired, use a little more crumpled tissue paper to add more drifts.

Load a feather with white paint which has the consistency of cream and pull a large, feathery vein across the board. Now take a Number 3 sable and pull some smaller veins through. Some of these should be placed in conjunction with the main vein; others can cross through or flow from it.

This finish does not seem to need such a high gloss finish to appear realistic. If used on a wall it is best left unvarnished. It is easily applied to a wall when laid out in squares to give the appearance of blocks of inlaid marble.

CRAYON BLACK AND WHITE MARBLE

This is a wonderfully resilient finish that becomes a fantasy glaze on almost any object. The recipe given in this chapter uses a grey glaze on a white background, but this procedure can be reversed if desired.

Materials:

- ✦ *One part japan or flat oil-based enamel paint*
- ✦ *One part scumbling medium*
- ✦ *One part mineral turpentine*
- ✦ *Compressed charcoal sticks*
- ✦ *Yellow Ochre pastel (not oil crayon)*
- ✦ *Sponges*
- ✦ *Oxhair brush*
- ✦ *38 mm cutter*
- ✦ *Tissue paper*
- ✦ *Cotton T-shirting*

Method: Pull a charcoal stick across the board, often laid on its side to give depth to the veins. Vary the intensity of the veins and pull back through the wide bands using the tip of the charcoal to create some thin veins. These should run parallel to and in conjunction with the initial veins.

Now wring out a sponge in water, dip it into the grey paint and sponge drifts onto the board. This is known as the 'major float' and should cover about seventy per cent of the surface. Take a cutter and blend, carrying some of the paint into the negative space and allowing some of the sponge impression to show up. If necessary, use a little cotton T-shirting to take off some paint, again removing it in drifts.

Take some crumpled tissue paper and fracture the surface in drifts. Using the coarse side of another sponge, load into white paint and apply some drifts of white. Form a pad with cotton T-shirting and carefully tamp up and down to blend slightly.

Stand back from the board and look at the marble from a distance. Decide which areas should have

CRAYON BLACK AND WHITE MARBLE

1. Draw veins on surface using pastels. 2. Apply grey glaze in drifts using a sponge wrung out in water. Cover about 70% of the board. Stipple to blend and take off a little with a piece of cotton T-shirting. Fracture with a crumpled tissue. 3. Using the coarse side of a sponge, apply white drifts. Tamp lightly with a cotton pad to blend. An overglaze can be applied after 24 hours. 4. A box or casket displays the completed finish.

GRANITE

1. Wring out sponge in water, load and lay on first drift.
2. Apply second colour in a drift.
3. Apply third colour. 4. Wring out sponge in mineral turpentine and blend the entire surface.
5. & 6. Office coffee table with granite finished top.

more paint removed or further application. If you decide to add a little more paint, re-load the sponge and quickly and lightly pounce on a little more. This will add a crystalline effect. Work quickly as by now the paint will be setting up. Allow to dry overnight and apply the overglaze.

Composition:

- ✦ *One part White, slightly greyed*
- ✦ *Nine parts mineral turpentine*

Mix up, paint quickly onto the whole surface and fracture all over with cotton T-shirting and tissue paper. This finish is excellent with a high gloss varnish, although two coats of satin and waxing will also give a good result.

GRANITE

This finish is executed on a black background so you will need first to coat a practice-board with three coats of semi-gloss black enamel paint. Normal preparation with flat oil-based enamel paint is used on a piece of furniture.

Materials:

- ✦ *Pale Grey*
- ✦ *Umbered Mid-Grey*
- ✦ *Deep Grey*
- ✦ *Sponges*
- ✦ *One part japan or flat oil-based enamel paint*
- ✦ *One part scumbling medium*
- ✦ *One part mineral turpentine*

Method: When this finish is used on a horizontal surface, the piece should first be coated in mineral turpentine. Exclude this step if working on a vertical surface. Remembering that all sponges should be first wrung out in water, dip sponge into the darkest grey and lay on drifts. Cover almost all of the board, allowing the black base colour to show through. Take the second sponge and load into the umbered grey and complete the same process covering slightly less area than the previous application.

With the third sponge apply the pale grey in drifts, using approximately the same volume as used in the previous sponging activity.

At this stage, if the finish appears a trifle pale,

sponge on some of the umbered grey or black. Now take a sponge and wring out in water, then in mineral turpentine. Lightly blend on the whole surface. The reticulation of the paint caused by the base application of mineral turpentine combined with this blending will pull the finish together and get rid of any harsh edges of paint. This may also be finished with a spatter of white or black.

Another good background colour for this finish is white, which combines well with the pink-beige and reddish tones seen in many granites. A gloss varnish is excellent for this stone finish.

MARBLE INLAY

This useful finish is quick, easy and well-suited to floors. Masonite or craftwood can be cut to fit the surface area, finished and then glued to the floor. When executing this finish for a floor take care to use extra strong marine varnishes, or cork tile varnish and apply up to ten coats. If the finish does become very scratched a professional sander can sand the floor before another coat of varnish is sprayed or painted on.

Materials:

- ✦ *One part japan or flat oil-based enamel paint*
- ✦ *One part scumbling medium*
- ✦ *One part mineral turpentine*
- ✦ *Oxhair brush*
- ✦ *Number 3 sable brush*
- ✦ *38 mm cutter*
- ✦ *Eraser with sharp edges*
- ✦ *Tissue paper*
- ✦ *Feathers*

Method: Lay out the board in the design shown by finding the centre of the board and marking out quarters and eighths. Mask in all the shapes. The first float of marble should then be run over the entire negative space, treating the board as one big block of marble which is to have other marbles inlaid. Make sure all the other areas of marble are blocked out so that the paint from this background marble does not spread.

The first marble may be a slightly beige-white colour. Try to ensure that the colours used in each marble are very close in shade as contrasting colours tend to give an unrealistic marbled look.

MARBLE INLAY

1. The design has been pencilled on and masked in. All internal sections are covered with paper or masking tape, including the centrepiece. Coat the negative space with mineral turpentine for reticulation. 2. Lay on first colour with a brush, stipple then feather veins all over the board. Stipple to blend. 3. For the centre panel, first brush on the lightest colour and stipple to remove brush strokes. Lay on the darkest colour with a feather.

4. Feather on the lighter colour, taking some into and beside the first feathering. 5. Use a clean feather loaded with turpentine to pull these veins out a little and to give a washy appearance. 6. You may wish to blend a little.

7. Negative veins may be pulled through by loading a sable brush with mineral turpentine and pulling through the finish before it is too set up. Roll brush between thumb and index finger as you pull. 8. Green marble for marble inlay has the following steps. First, paint on green, stipple to remove brush strokes. Second, use small pieces of crumpled tissue paper to create drifts. Third, create negative veins by pulling off paint using a mineral turpentine laden sable brush or an eraser. Paint on a few thin black veins as accents. In this picture the board is still masked but the finishes are completed. 9. The finished inlay board.

GREEN MARBLE

Green Marble
1. Apply the glaze all over the board and quickly stipple to remove the brush strokes. Roughly run a plastic bag and a crumpled newspaper over the surface to create a drift. Dry overnight. 2. Wring out sponge in water and apply the second glaze. Fracture with more tissue paper. Sponge and lightly pull over the board so that the finish is slightly blurred. Now blur the edges with cotton T-shirting. 3. The next day you may wish to add some very pale and thinned drifts of white with a sponge. 4. Vein with a feather and sable brushes, blurring and blotting the veins and reapplying colour in some areas to add depth. 5. Green marble, a superb table finish, edged in bronze powder stencilling.

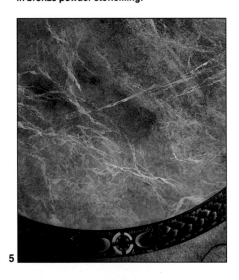

FANTASY MARBLE

1. Using a feather lay on the first float (white) in drifts covering about three quarters of the surface. Then float on the second colour, leaving a little negative space here and there. 2. Blend with a stipple brush, light into dark, dark into light. 3. If desired, add veins with a sable brush or feather.

Fantasy marble finish on standard lamp and shade.

Coat the entire negative space with the off-beige colour. Quickly stipple with the cutter or stipple brush to remove any brush strokes. Load a feather into a deeper shade of beige and run diagonal veins across the board. Briefly forget the masked pieces and imagine just a 60 cm x 60 cm block of marble. The diagonal should run one way right across the board with occasional smaller drifts running off in other directions. Blend carefully with the cutter, making sure you wipe it off all the time. Take some of the accent colour into the lighter space and some of the background colour into the darker areas. All the colours should remain defined.

Dry overnight and lift the tape which had masked out the areas for the darker pinkish marble. Apply an isolating coat of shellac to the existing marble. Remember to mask in around the outside edges of this area to ensure that the paint does not spread onto the main piece of marble.

For the pink marble you will need three shades ranging from dark to light. First brush on the lightest colour with an oxhair brush, and stipple to remove brush strokes. Using a feather, lay on a diagonal vein in the darkest shade of pink, then feather on the second colour in a vein, taking some into and beside the first vein. Load a clean feather with mineral turpentine to pull these veins out a little and create a slightly washy appearance. You may wish to blend just a very little with the cutter.

For a Green Serpentine effect, the areas should be masked out as above. Paint on the green paint and stipple to remove any brush strokes. Take a tiny piece of crumpled tissue paper and fracture in some drifts. With the edge of an eraser pull through some negative veins, some largish, some very tiny and interlocking. If any appear too strong simply stipple a little green into them. Use a Number 3 sable to lay in a few heavier black veins.

GREEN MARBLE

For this finish, the practice board should have already been coated in a bright green semi-gloss enamel, or for furniture the obligatory five coats of flat enamel paint should have been applied. The piece should already have been wet-sanded and isolated. (See Chapter 2.)

Materials:

- *One part japan or flat oil-based enamel paint*
- *One part scumbling medium*
- *One part mineral turpentine*
- *Sponges*
- *Feathers*
- *Cotton T-shirting*
- *Number 3 sable brush*

Method: The first glaze is dark green. Apply the glaze all over the board with a large brush and stipple to remove brush stokes. Roughly run a plastic bag over the surface and use some crumpled newspaper to make a drift. This should be left to dry overnight.

Using a sponge which has been wrung out in water, apply drifts of the second glaze in pale green and then fracture with tissue paper. Apply more of the pale green with a sponge, hitting the finish with the sponge and then lightly pulling it on the board so that the surface is slightly blurred. This technique should represent drifts only. Now take some cotton t-shirting and apply it softly, carefully blurring some of the edges of the sponging.

Allow to dry overnight and apply veins using white with a little green added. Use a feather and a Number 3 sable. The veins should receive a lot of blotting with cotton t-shirting. More colour can be applied over the top in some areas so that the veins appear to sink into the marble. This finish looks best when coated with gloss varnish.

FANTASY MARBLE

This is a very useful finish for small surfaces.

Materials:

- *One part japan or oil based enamel paint*
- *One part scumbling medium*
- *One part mineral turpentine*
- *Feathers*
- *38 mm cutter or stipple brush*

Method: Float on the main colour using a feather to cover about three-quarters of the board. Using another feather, float on the contrast colour, leaving a tiny amount of negative space here and there. Blend with the cutter or stipple brush, light into dark, dark into light and some colour into the negative space. Be very careful not to produce a muddy looking finish. Coat with flat, satin or gloss varnish.

10

CRACKLE FINISH

CRACKLE MEDIUM, a modern paint finish, is an exciting and unusual finish to add to your repertoire. The application of two incompatible substances creates a unique cracked paint surface which can be either exaggerated or refined. A heavy, graphic finish is generally suited to larger contemporary pieces while a fine, subtle look can be imparted on small or old items. Alternatively old cracked paint and varnish finishes, particularly those of the 'japanned' style, popular during the eighteenth and nineteenth centuries, can be simulated using cracklure. Cracklure is also composed of two incompatible substances which leave a transparent cracked layer over the surface of the piece. To add to the cracked, aged effect of cracklure, you can then rub colour into the finish.

Detail of cracklure and design in gold leaf on mirror pictured on previous page.

THIS FINISH, which gives the impression of surface cracking through age, seems to have a certain mystique attached to it. It is an extremely useful finish and can be modified or extended to give a host of varying aged effects. Before tackling a piece of furniture, practise on several sample boards to achieve the finish you desire. The first finish using Cracklure, dries clear and gives a series of fine, cobweb-like cracks. The second finish is composed of a base called Crackle Medium and water-based paint which can be mixed to any colour. Cracklure and Crackle Medium are available from specialty stockists. (See page 156.)

CRACKLURE

It is important first to consider the piece to be finished. Cracklure imparts an aged appearance which does not suit all contemporary shapes. Ideally, it will complement shapes from eighteenth and nineteenth centuries, using base colours of red, black, dark green and blue. The darker the colour, the more successful the finish. Your piece should already have been painted, wet-sanded and varnished with two coats of satin varnish so that the surface to be cracked is not porous. If it is porous the Cracklure will be absorbed and cracking will not appear.

Plastic chain store jug, completely transformed with a crackle finish and gold leaf trim.

White plastic waste paper bin has been treated with a pink crackle finish and a hand-painted bow.

Method: Using an oxhair brush, carefully apply the Cracklure base coat. If necessary, thin with mineral turpentine so that it flows on more easily. It is absolutely imperative that the application is uniform so there is no uneven drying which will affect the application of the top coat of Cracklure. Allow to dry from thirty minutes to two-and-a-half hours, depending on the weather. Watch carefully as the drying time can be very tricky. Some pieces begin to dry immediately with the result that the second medium can be applied almost straight away. With others, a longer drying time is necessary. To test for dryness, use the trick of applying a clean, dry knuckle to the surface. If a clicking sound is heard on pulling the knuckle away, the piece is ready to take the second medium. Do not allow fingers to come into contact with the surface as finger marks cannot be eradicated from the finish. This first medium is compatible with mineral turpentine and the brush should be washed in the normal fashion.

Apply the second medium with extreme care. It is not possible to work the brush backwards and forwards across the base medium as it may be disturbed. Carefully lay the medium over as quickly and as gently as possible. Cracking should start occurring almost immediately. The second medium is water-based so the brush can simply be washed in hot soapy water. Allow the piece to dry overnight.

The next day the piece can be aged further by rubbing with rottenstone then wiping off. Two protective coats of flat or satin varnish are necessary, followed by a good waxing. Alternatively, try a stain glaze of one part flat black (or white, depending on the base colour) oil-based enamel paint and two parts mineral turpentine. Paint all over the piece and wipe off, using a cotton cloth. The paint will stain the cracks giving a rich, antiqued effect. Finish with two coats of satin or flat varnish and wax.

You can create your own celadon glaze by painting an object with celadon green paint, applying the two mediums as above and finally rubbing a white stain glaze made up of one part white flat oil-based enamel paint and two parts mineral turpentine into the cracklure. Wipe off with a cotton cloth and apply two coats of satin varnish as a final finish.

CRACKLE MEDIUM

This is a viscous, clear, sticky fluid which creates very graphic cracking. The paint for this finish may be in any colour but it must be water-based. The consistency of the paint should be reasonably thick rather than runny. The thicker the paint, the bigger the cracks. Brushes are washed out in soapy water.

Because of its dramatic effect, crackle medium is best suited to contemporary pieces. Pieces with already prepared surfaces such as parsons' tables, coffee tables, bookshelves or plastic wastebins make perfect subjects.

CRACKLE FINISH

1. Apply crackle medium. Allow to dry for 1-2 hours or overnight. The medium should be touch-dry. 2. Apply water-based paint very carefully, without stopping and starting. Use straight and even strokes. Do not come back over the finish with the brush. The brush must slide over the crackle medium. 3. The finish cracks as soon as it starts to dry.

1

2

3

A basic department store table, left, looks entirely different with the addition of a crackle medium finish. Cream was laid over a blue background with decorative blue striping. A Celadon finish using cracklure lifts a simple glass vase, right. Note the fine detail in the finish, below.

Make sure there is plenty of paper beneath the piece about to receive the finish as the medium tends to run and can be messy. The piece should have been prepared in the usual way and the surface on which the medium is to be applied should be non-porous.

Method: Apply the crackle medium with a nylon brush, or 10 cm foam pad if it is a large piece. On commercially prepared pieces, such as tables, ceramic lamp bases, or vases the medium can run and turn lacy. If this occurs once the first coat is dry, apply another coat, making sure that any holes are covered. Take care to catch any drips as they will show up in the final finish if left. The usual drying time for this finish is about two to four hours, but overnight is preferable.

When applying the water-based paint, use a brush suitable for the size of the piece — either the small nylon brush or large foam pad. If the surface area is large it will be impossible to apply the paint in long straight strokes as a definite mark is left where the paint runs out and where the brush is re-loaded. Do not work the brush backwards and forwards across the medium. The strokes must go on and that is it. If you start to work the brush backwards and forwards the medium beneath will be disturbed and you will end up with a frightful mess. Use a series of short strokes, in a basketweave pattern. Apply one stroke at an angle to the edge of the piece and then apply the next stroke at right angles to the first stroke. Work quickly as the paint begins to dry and crack immediately. On a small piece the application of the paint with a nylon brush is more simple and straight strokes can be used successfully. When dry spectacular cracking will have appeared.

A fine, cobwebby cracking can be created by spraying the paint with water from a mister immediately following application. The piece is ready for a coat of varnish and if desired, a positive or negative stipple with an antiquing glaze. This would be in the normal mixture of one part japan paint and one part scumbling medium, and turpentine as desired. (See Chapter 3.) Remember that it is most important to seal with a coat of varnish before applying an antiquing glaze as the finish is extremely delicate and may pull off if it contacts another substance.

FINAL FINISH

As already mentioned, it is most important that the finish should receive a coat of varnish before any work such as an antiquing glaze is applied. I have found that it is also extremely difficult to stripe this finish. The safest way is to stripe negatively. Once the crackle medium has dried, lay down masking tape where you wish to have a stripe. There is no forgiveness with this operation — once the tape is down it must be left. If you try to remove it the crackle medium will come away too. So be very careful. Apply the paint to the crackle medium, leaving the tape as visible as possible. When the paint has dried, take an X-acto knife and very carefully run it along the edge of the tape making sure you cut through the water-based paint and the crackle medium. Now lift the tape and the base colour becomes your stripe.

This is how the table (on page 126) was striped. In order to give the table protection as it was to be used constantly, I applied ten coats of high gloss varnish. The wet-sanding was executed then two coats of satin varnish were applied. Although Crackle finish is quick and easy, it does require many coats of protective varnish.

127

11

SHAGREEN

Naive-designed boxes grace a scallop-edged craftwood table which has been finished in shagreen. Shagreen is a rare finish which takes its name from an ancient form of specially treated asses and sharks' skin.

THE USE OF SHARKSKIN to cover small decorative ornaments such as boxes, tea caddies, cigarette tins and jewel cases has been in vogue since the seventeenth century. Today the same objects have become prized possessions of collectors. The technique explained in this chapter offers a simple way of simulating these valuable pieces. Using quick, simple and inexpensive methods you can achieve this rare and exotic look on your own pieces.

1

2

3

4

A butler's tray finished in shagreen and aged silver leaf.

1. Apply the glaze with an oxhair brush 2. Stipple to remove brush strokes. 3. Spray with water to open up papillae-like indentations. 4. Use a cotton bud to remove a little paint here and there.

THE UNTANNED LEATHER from which shagreen takes its name was textured by the stamping-in of seeds which were trampled into the hides when they were still moist and shaken out when they had dried, leaving small granular indentations. The leather was then stained. The name shagreen is also applied to the finely granulated skin of sharks and sting rays, ground flat so that the pearl-like *papillae* of the skin form a granulated pattern. This skin has been used since the seventeenth century to make decorative and functional objects.

Shagreen, as well as being extremely popular during the eighteenth century, had a resurgence of use during the Art Deco period when it was often used to cover tables and chairs in the traditional colours of grey, green, pink and blue.

To create your own shagreen finish start with a simple small piece which has been coated with five coats of base colour. (See Chapter 2.) The colour should be white and slightly tinted with the final colour you intend to use on the piece. Apply the wet-sanding and isolating process as explained in Chapter 2.

Materials:

- **One part flat japan paint**
- **One part scumbling medium**
- **One part mineral turpentine**
- **Plant mister filled with water**
- **Oxhair brush**
- **Stipple brush**

Method: Paint the glaze on with an oxhair brush and stipple to remove brush strokes. Spray with water from a plant mister. If you are working on a vertical surface be careful not to spray too much water as this will run on the finish. The important activity in this technique is to spray the water with enough force to open up the paint and leave the circular marks which characterise real shagreen.

The water should be allowed to remain on the

A restored knife box finished in shagreen with oxidised silver leaf trims.

surface in blobs until it evaporates. It will do this on a vertical surface if sprayed on in just enough quantity. If necessary, take a cotton bud and remove a little paint in a slightly irregular pattern to give more authenticity to the finish.

When the water has evaporated the piece is ready to be varnished. This finish is very resistant to varnish and the first coats are difficult to apply. If the piece is a table which is to be used regularly, apply four to six coats of high gloss, wet-sand and then apply two coats of satin varnish. For a small decorative piece, two coats of varnish will suffice. The piece should then be waxed.

131

12

WALL GLAZES

WALL GLAZES, PROPERLY PREPARED and applied, can add extra dimension, warmth and soft illusory qualities to small or awkwardly-shaped rooms. Originally developed by the master painters of the sixteenth and seventeenth centuries, glazing techniques were later taken up by decorative painters who applied their talents to the furniture, walls and ceilings of houses and public buildings. The wall glazes used today are based on similar methods, with each glaze following basic rules of composition. Each simply consists of a transparent layer of colour laid in a thin coat over an opaque surface. The colour is then variously built up or applied using different methods to create desired visual foils and depth. Having chosen a wall glaze, you may wish to apply a separate finish to skirting boards. The Breche, Black marble, Dragging and Parchment finishes in this chapter have been developed for this purpose.

133

A S WITH ALL SURFACES which are to receive a painted finish, preparation is mandatory for all wall glazes. If a wall has not been prepared properly, any flaws or irregularities will stand out and ruin the final finish. Make sure that cracks are filled, allowed to dry, sanded and then re-filled. When dried a second time, sand back so that they blend perfectly smoothly with the wall. Once this is completed and the wall is completely smooth and clean, apply one coat of oil-based sealer. This will prevent the filler showing up in dark splotches through the finish and absorbing any wall glaze.

Before the first coat of paint is applied, the wall should be sanded down with 220 sandpaper, dusted off and wiped over with a tack cloth. It will help if the room environment as well as the wall surface is dry and clean. Any dirt or dampness will prevent the paint from sticking, so it is necessary to keep cleaning the room as you work. The principles of preparation described in Chapter 2 apply similarly to walls; the scale of operation is simply larger.

Now coat the walls with three applications of eggshell paint, which is half flat oil-based enamel mixed with half semi-gloss oil-based enamel. The walls should be prepared with flat oil or water-based paint only if you intend to use a wall glaze that requires an absorbent base, eg Fresco.

Each coat should be carefully sanded with 220 sandpaper and be just as carefully dusted off. Clean and vacuum the room and wipe over the walls with a tack cloth before the wall glaze is applied. The eggshell finish gives exactly the same surface as a piece of furniture which has been prepared following the directions for preparation given in Chapter 2.

For a room 3 x 3 metres square usually one litre of mixed colour combined with one litre scumbling medium and one or more litres of mineral turpentine will be sufficient. However, if you are just starting on wall glazing, it is wise to mix much more.

Mix two litres of colour then mix together just one litre each of scumbling medium, paint and mineral turpentine. This means that you will not waste the scumbling medium if you do manage to complete the room with the smaller quantity. You still have the safeguard of having an extra litre of colour available if you need it. Even for the expert, it is very difficult to re-mix the exact colour so it is not advisable for the

134

amateur to have to try re-mixing a colour to match.

It is also worth noting that techniques can change from day to day. Therefore, try to complete the whole room in one day. If only two walls are completed on one day and the remaining two the next day, it is quite possible that the surfaces will look quite different.

To slow down drying time you can add safflower oil to the glaze. That is, one-quarter of the entire volume of paint, scumbling medium and mineral turpentine may be safflower oil. Any triple refined oil will suffice. Be aware however that safflower oil will repel varnish.

Kerosene can also be used to slow down drying time. Replace part or all of the mineral turpentine with kerosene. Beware of the fumes and remember that kerosene renders the paint surface very fragile.

FRESCO

This is a three step wall finish in which first a water-based paint is washed onto a wall prepared with off-white flat water-based or oil-based paint, either of which must be flat and absorbent.

Using a 38 mm cutter, apply the deepest-toned water-based paint in drifts using a wet sponge and cheesecloth to texture and move around the wall. When the first application is dry (about one hour), apply the second glaze, an off-white oil-based colour which should be thin enough to allow the base coat to glow through. Apply in drifts with a brush and texture with a wet sponge and cheesecloth. If desired, the finish can be left at this stage. Otherwise, the third step involves the application of a coat of thinned oil-based ochre paint. Wash it onto about 90 per cent of the surface and again apply texture using a wet sponge and cheesecloth. This technique can be used in any combination of colours you desire.

SIMPLE FRESCO

This finish is used on walls which require a quick, efficient restoration finish. Simple fresco quickly gives a new look to walls which are clean, though slightly rough and porous. Japan paint, used straight from the can, is excellent to use because of its viscosity. Take the paint, load it onto cheesecloth and rub into the walls very roughly in a circular motion. Now wet the cheesecloth liberally with mineral tur-

Trompe l'oeil or 'trick of the eye' is a special technique of painting realistic scenes. Simple to learn, it is also complemented by marble paint finishes used as wall glazes.

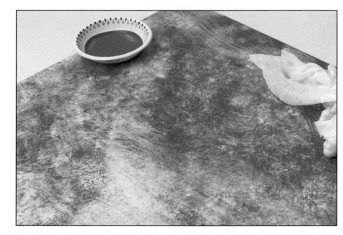
1. Using a 38mm cutter, apply colour in drifts. Take a wet sponge and cheesecloth, then create texture, moving around the wall.

2. When the first application has dried for about one hour, apply the second glaze, an off-white colour which should be thin enough to allow the base to glow through. The finish can now be completed, if desired.

3. The third glaze, thinned yellow ochre, is washed on to give about 90 per cent coverage. This is textured with cheesecloth and sponge.

SIMPLE FRESCO

1. Take japan or other oil-based paint straight out of the can and onto cheesecloth. Rub very roughly into the walls using a circular motion. 2. Wet cheesecloth liberally with mineral turpentine and rub over the paint, giving a full and even colour on the walls. 3. Take another piece of cheesecloth, wet with mineral turpentine and start slapping over the paint surface to create texture. If you want more colour, re-load the original cloth and texture over the walls. 4. This finish is excellent when waxed, however the paint must be dried for two or three weeks before working. Mix carnauba wax with burnt umber and rub well into the paint surface. Buff off with a soft cloth. 5. Or, using the mix of carnauba wax and burnt umber, stipple evenly all over the wall. After some weeks this dries to a hard surface and may be buffed.

1

2

3

4

5

pentine and rub over the paint to give a full but uneven colour on the walls. Take another piece of cheesecloth, wet with mineral turpentine and start slapping it over the paint surface again to add texture. If more colour is required load some paint onto the original piece of cheesecloth and apply to the walls. When the wall surface has dried for twenty-four hours it can be waxed either with plain wax or wax mixed with burnt or raw umber. This is a quick, simple and very effective wall glaze.

SINGLE PROCESS BAGGING

The wall should be prepared in eggshell oil-based enamel paint, white or whatever pale background colour is desired.

Materials:

+ *One part flat oil-based enamel or japan paint*
+ *One part scumbling medium*

+ *One or two parts mineral turpentine*
+ *Large plastic bags cut open down the side and base*

Method: Paint or roll the glaze over one wall and apply texture with the plastic bag as described in the following recipe for Double Process Bagging.

DOUBLE PROCESS BAGGING

This glaze uses red, blue and grey japan paints. Texture is added using a plastic bag.

Materials:

+ *Red and blue japan paint*
+ *One part flat oil-based enamel or japan paint*
+ *One part scumbling medium*
+ *One or two parts mineral turpentine*

+ *Large plastic garbage bag cut open down the side and base*
+ *Cheesecloth*
+ *Large painters' brushes*

Method: Prepare the wall with off-white eggshell oil-based paint. Load two pieces of cheesecloth with the red and blue paints straight from the can and rub onto the wall in cloud-like drifts. You may prefer to lay one

SINGLE PROCESS BAGGING

1. Quickly paint or roll the glaze over the wall.

2. Texture with plastic bags which have been slightly crumpled. Run your hand over the surface and then squash bag into a ball and retexture.

colour first and then come back with the second. The effect should resemble amorphous clouds scudding across the wall. Dry overnight and then paint or roll on the grey glaze (composed as above).

Two people must work together. One rolls while the other applies texture. About 1.2 metres should be rolled on quickly then textured. Make sure the edge is kept wet so that there is no join mark. Always roll the outside edge irregularly so that if there is a join mark it is not a straight line. Have plenty of bags on hand. They cannot be re-used as they will redistribute the paint. The person texturing must lay a bag on the wall, slightly crumpling the surface and rubbing with a flat hand. Remove the bag and continue with a new bag. If desired, return with plastic bag squashed into a ball and pounce lightly to give more texture.

137

DOUBLE PROCESS BAGGING

1. This glaze uses three colours. Lay on the two base colours in amorphous, cloud-like drifts. Dry overnight. 2. Paint or roll on grey glaze. Quickly texture with a plastic bag, laying it on the wall slightly crumpled. Run your hand over the surface. Remove and continue the process. You may wish then to squash the plastic bag into a ball and again texture the surface.

RAG ROLLING

1. Roll or paint the glaze onto the wall and run the rolled up cotton cloth across the surface. 2. The result gives a very satisfactory texture.

STIPPLING

1. Roll or brush the paint on in 1 to 1¼ metre strips, keeping a wet edge. Two people should be working, one painting and one stippling. If you are working alone, apply the paint in an "S" shape so that no join marks will show. 2. Stipple with an up and down motion, making sure the brush does not turn on the paint surface.

RAG ROLLING

Rag rolling is one of the most popular and easiest of the wall glazes to learn. Softly twisted cloths are pressed into a wet glaze to leave a dappled flow of colour. The walls should be prepared using eggshell oil-based enamel paint. The same texture of cloth should be used all the time, as a variety of textures will change the patterns imposed on the walls. The most successful way to do this is to buy cheesecloth or sheeting and cut into almost one metre lengths and then wash and dry. It is most important that any dressing is removed from the material.

Materials:

+ *One part flat oil-based enamel or japan paint*
+ *One part scumbling medium*
+ *One or two parts mineral turpentine*
+ *Roller*
+ *Absorbent cotton cloths, eg T-shirting or towels*

Method: Rag rolling is done by folding the cloth diagonally, rolling it into a twist and folding it in two. The paint is rolled or painted onto the wall and the sausage of cloth is quickly rolled across the paint, changing direction often so that there are no straight lines. Make sure the whole wall is textured and that no large patches of colour are left untreated. As soon as the cloth becomes covered in paint it must be discarded and a new piece used.

RAGGING

This finish is created simply by using bunched up cloths to texture the paint glaze.

Method: Using the same ingredients as for Rag Rolling paint or roll glaze onto the wall and quickly texture with a dry cloth. The cloth must be discarded as soon as it becomes clogged with paint.

Alternatively, soak a large number of cloths in mineral turpentine, wring out and store in a plastic bag to retain moisture. Paint or roll the glaze onto the wall and texture with the moist cloths. This will create quite a graphic effect, giving more scope to create light and shade. It also enables you to blend the join marks and keep a wet edge with greater ease.

Another method is to soak the cloths in a mix of 50 per cent scumbling medium and 50 per cent mineral turpentine, wring them out and store in plastic bags. Roll or paint on the glaze and texture with the cloth.

STIPPLING

Materials:

+ *One part flat oil-based enamel or japan paint*
+ *One part scumbling medium*
+ *One part mineral turpentine*
+ *Roller or paint brush*
+ *Wall stipple brush*

Method: The wall should be prepared with eggshell oil-based enamel paint. Roll the glaze evenly onto the wall and pounce the stippling brush up and down exactly as instructed in Chapter 3. In this instance, however, a proper painters' stippling brush is necessary unless the wall surface is small and easily managed with a smaller round stipple brush.

DRAGGING

Materials:

+ *One part flat oil-based enamel or japan paint*
+ *One part scumbling medium*
+ *One or two parts mineral turpentine*
+ *Roller or paint brush*

Method: The wall should be prepared with eggshell oil-based enamel paint. This gives a good graphic appearance. A proper painters' dragging brush is the best tool to give a fine graphic quality to the glaze. For a fine, silken finish, place a piece of cotton over the brush and then pull the brush through the glaze.

To obtain fine, graduated lines from one end of the wall to the other the glaze should be rolled on evenly. It is essential to work with another person to do this. One person can work from a ladder pulling the brush through the glaze and the second person can wait below to take the brush without allowing it to waver, and continue the sweep down the wall. Although this activity can be quite tricky, it is well worth the effort. Pull the brush down through the glaze from top to bottom, feathering out at the bottom and making one more sweep to the top. An alternative silken effect

effect can be created the next day by rolling on a white stain glaze (90 per cent mineral turpentine, 10 per cent paint) containing a little of the wall glaze colour and pulling the brush through in the same way.

SPONGING

The sponge is a wonderful tool which can be used to apply a number of layers or colours, building up a great depth of paint. Follow the directions given for sponging in Chapter 3. Practise using colour combinations on a sample board, then move on to your walls. It is always wise to keep the contrast between the wall colour and the glaze colour low.

SIMPLE MARBLE

This wall glaze consists of greyed white and pale grey with a slightly deeper grey used as an accent colour like the marble in the Marble Inlay in Chapter 9. The colours should be very close together so that there is not too much overall contrast.

Materials:

+ *One part flat oil-based enamel or japan paint*
+ *One part scumbling medium*
+ *One or two parts mineral turpentine*

+ *38 mm cutter, or larger such as the wall stipple brush (depending on the dimensions of the wall)*

Method: The wall should first be prepared with white eggshell oil-based enamel paint. Using a brush, lay on the major float of slightly greyed white in big open drifts that cover about three-quarters of the wall. Take a second brush and lay grey drifts in conjunction with the first float. The volume must be less than the first application as this is simply an accent to the original float. Quickly lay in the darker grey accent drifts. Make sure that these two accent floats are laid in with some length, width and movement. One of the great disasters that can occur in this finish is that the accent strokes can be too short, wriggly and wormlike, giving a busy, dazzling appearance. Now blend with a cutter or wall stipple brush so that there are no harsh outlines. For further instructions, see Chapter 9.

CHECKLIST
1. After a tin of scumbling medium has been opened, always place two or more pieces of aluminium foil and then cling wrap immediately on the liquid. This will seal the liquid and stop a skin from forming. Skin forms very quickly and it can be quite thick, resulting in a loss of large amounts of the medium once it is removed.
2. The same operation applies to paint, particularly if the paint is not used regularly. Pour some mineral turpentine over the paint, place a piece of cling wrap right down over the top and then place a second piece of cling wrap over that to keep the air away from the paint.

SKIRTING BOARDS

Skirting boards as well as walls can receive decorative finishes. If the skirting boards are new they must be sanded then sealed with a commercial sealer. Two coats of thinned semi-gloss off-white enamel should then be applied. Older skirting boards should be well sanded, filled if necessary, sealed and painted with two to three coats of thinned semi-gloss enamel.

SERPENTINE GREEN

Materials:

+ *One part green japan paint (see Colour Recipe No 1)*
+ *One part scumbling medium*
+ *One part mineral turpentine*

+ *Sponge*
+ *Black flat oil-based paint*
+ *Tissue paper*
+ *Sharp sided eraser*

Method: Paint on green and quickly stipple to remove brush strokes. Wring out a sponge in water then dip into black paint and paint on a series of 'W' shapes over the green. Stipple slightly to blend. Fracture here and there with crumpled tissue paper. Now take an eraser and, holding it on an edge, pull through a series of veins, more rather than a few. If some veins are too graphic, stipple a little of the green into them. This may be finished with a coat of satin varnish if desired.

DRAGGING

1. Paint or roll the glaze onto the wall. Two people should work at this process. 2. Pull dragging brush down wall, feathering out at the bottom. Then pull brush up from the bottom and feather out at the top. 3. For a silken effect, cover the brush with cotton. This gives a softer, less graphic result.

SIMPLE MARBLE

1. Lay the major float on the wall (greyed white) in big open drifts covering about three quarters of the wall. With a second brush lay in dark grey drifts in conjunction with the first float, but in much smaller volumes. 2. Blend with a stipple brush or cutter. Beware of creating a muddy finish.

141

SERPENTINE GREEN

1. Paint on green and stipple to remove any brush strokes. 2. Load a sponge with black and create a series of 'W' shapes. 3. Pull through negative veins using an eraser. 4. Re-texture with crumpled tissue paper to remove too graphic a look.

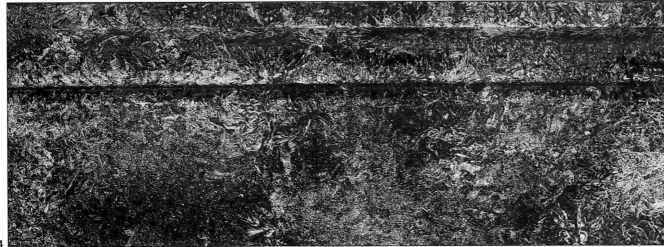

BRÊCHE

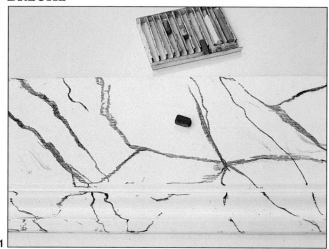

1. Draw on veins using compressed charcoal or pastels. 2. Paint on grey glaze and stipple to remove any brush strokes. 3. Wring out chamois in water and remove stone-like shapes from the grey glaze. 4. Load a dampened sponge with white and lay on some drifts while blending slightly to reduce harshness of the effect.

BLACK MARBLE

  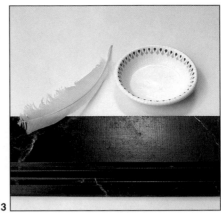

1. Apply drifts of white with a dampened sponge. 2. Break up drifts and remove some paint with a cotton cloth. 3. Lay on white veins with a feather.

DRAGGING

  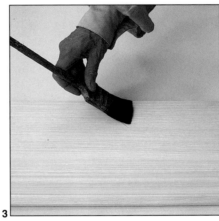

1. Paint on the glaze, in the given recipe of one third each of paint, scumbling medium and mineral turpentine. 2. Texture in a sideways movement with cotton. 3. Detail dragging with a 38mm cutter.

BRÊCHE

Brêche is named after the marble of the same name which has large, sometimes dramatic formations of stone running through it.

Materials:

- ✦ *One part Umbered Grey japan or flat oil-based paint*
- ✦ *One part scumbling medium*
- ✦ *One or two parts mineral turpentine*
- ✦ *Sticks of compressed charcoal*
- ✦ *Chamois*
- ✦ *Oxhair brush*
- ✦ *38 mm cutter*

Method: The skirting board is prepared with an off-white semi-gloss enamel paint. A slight umber grey is used for the glaze. Using a piece of compressed charcoal, draw veins across the skirting board, inter-locking and varying them to look thin, wide, large and small. Paint on the grey glaze and stipple to remove brush strokes. Wring out the chamois in water and apply to the paint in order to remove large stone-like shapes from the glaze. Keep re-folding the chamois so that the same shape is not repeated.

When this is completed, wring out a sponge in water and load lightly with white paint which has the consistency of cream. Apply some drifts and then attempt to apply further fractures to the surface with crumpled tissue paper.

BLACK MARBLE

For a black marble skirting board, prepare the surface with two or three thinned coats of semi-gloss black enamel paint. Use exactly the same technique as for Quick Black Marble described in Chapter 9. This finish looks magnificent in an all-white room with few pieces of furniture.

DRAGGING

Materials:

- ✦ *One part japan or flat oil-based paint*
- ✦ *One part scumbling medium*
- ✦ *One part mineral turpentine*
- ✦ *Cheesecloth or cotton*
- ✦ *Oxhair brush*
- ✦ *38 mm cutter*

Method: This finish may be applied in any colour, after the skirting board surface has first been coated in two thinned coats of off-white semi-gloss enamel. Start on one side of a doorway and work around the room so that the finish is completed at the other side of the doorway. By using this method you will avoid the messy join that can occur where two walls meet.

Paint on the antiquing glaze and quickly drag with a bunched up piece of T-shirting or cheesecloth. Take a dry stiff-bristled brush and a 38 mm cutter and detail.

PARCHMENT

Materials:

- ✦ *One part japan or flat oil-based paint*
- ✦ *One part scumbling medium*
- ✦ *One part mineral turpentine*
- ✦ *38 mm cutter*
- ✦ *Stipple brush*
- ✦ *Cheesecloth*

Method: Paint all over skirting board and apply texture while also taking off some paint with cheesecloth. If necessary, stipple a little to blend.

A simple design, hand-painted on the wall in an apartment dining room, highlights a decorative collection of tableware. This design was executed in two hours.

13

LIMING

Here are a number of pieces of furniture with a limed finish. The pine table received a traditional finish of three coats of white liming medium, painted on and then wiped off. The oak frame, redeemed from a second-hand shop, was finished in the same manner, with the addition of a thin layer of pale green painted around the outside and inner edges.

The craftwood lampbase, shelves and wastepaper basket were first painted with colour, distressed and then finished with coats of wiped-off liming medium. The pig received a full coating of spakfilla which was then sanded off. The table was given a coat of four coats of water-based, water-clear floor varnish for protection.

FOR THIS PROCESS, obviously, the wood should have open pores or grain, although it is possible to create the appearance of liming on solid surfaces such as craftwood, as you can see from the photographs. If you are liming pine, then you should rub the pine with a wire brush which will help create the effect of grain and will also cause the softer areas of the wood to lie in relief. Cedar and pitch pine may be treated in the same way.

The wood should be raw, i.e. all paint or vanish must be removed. If liming a floor, good sanding and preparation is imperative. Do not, under any circumstances, hire a sanding machine and attempt the job on the floor yourself.

The machines, which are available for hire, in the hands of an amateur tend to become uncontrollable and gouge out areas of wood and generally create an unseemly mess of your floor. Spend the money—and bring in a professional to sand your floor.

Once the floor is sanded, the room cleaned of all dust (that means working all over the room with cotton cloths, followed by tack rags), the raw wood must be sealed with shellac. If you do not seal the wood you will find that the liming will disappear in a year or two, soaked up by the raw wood. Shellac provides a base which is still porous enough to hold the paint, but stops the paint soaking into the wood completely.

About two litres of shellac will seal a floor 4.5m x 4.5m. When the shellac is dry (about twenty minutes) place a piece of 220 sandpaper on the end of a squeegee, or broom and sand the floor, changing the sandpaper frequently. Vacuum the floor and room to remove any dust. This same principle is applied to small decorative pieces and furniture.

If working on a piece of furniture, make sure your sanding is perfect, so that the piece has a wonderful tactile quality as well as visual beauty.

When you are ready to commence liming, you may choose to use a commercial liming medium or flat oil-based enamel. The liming medium is specially prepared so that it has a built-in degree of translucency which is most desirable. The liming medium also stays 'open' longer than straight paint, enabling you to have more working time and helping to eliminate join marks which often occur on floors.

If you choose to use flat white enamel, thin slightly with mineral turpentine, paint on to the piece of furniture and then gently wipe off with a cotton cloth. It is for you to decide how much colour you wish to remove. When the layer of paint is dry (overnight) you may wish to remove a little more colour and this is achieved by again sanding with 220 sandpaper. You may wish to add another layer of paint and so on until you have achieved the desired effect. On furniture, usually three applications will suffice. Once again, the decision is yours, the more layers you apply, the more depth you create.

1. Sand the raw pine with 220 sandpaper, seal with shellac, and sand again. Paint on the white liming medium, and wipe off with a cotton cloth. Allow to dry overnight.

The next day, paint on a second coat of white liming medium. If you wish to have a very subtle effect, wipe off with a cotton cloth. (The second coat was left untouched in this photo.)

For a very solid, opaque limed effect, a third coat of liming medium was painted on on the third day. For protection use a water-based floor finish.

You may wish to start with a colour initially. If so, simply thin japan or flat enamel with mineral turpentine OR tint the liming medium with japan or flat enamel. The colour is painted on and wiped off then left to dry (overnight). If you are wanting to add yet another colour it is wise to isolate the first coat with a coat of shellac or water-based varnish (for quick drying) before the second application. As the colour is thinly applied it is possible that in brushing on and removing some of the second coat of colour, some of the first colour is pulled off. The isolation coat prevents this happening.

A lovely application of colour on furniture is white, eau-de-nil and white and to take this a step further, you can then paint on pink followed by a final application of white. Each step, if this is executed on a piece of furniture, should be lightly sanded with 220 sandpaper which gives the piece a wonderful tactile quality. It is very labour intensive, but gives a fabulous effect on furniture. The finish would then be protected with two or three coats of water-based, water-clear floor varnish.

A quick, commercial painter's trick of liming is to load a piece of cotton with the liming medium or flat enamel and lightly run on to the piece. This gives a very good effect, and is quick and relatively easy.

When liming a piece with very obvious grain or open pores you may wish the grain to be even more prominent. This may be achieved by painting on filler and sanding off when dry. The white will remain solidly in the pores of the wood. You can then lime over the piece, and the pores will show up quite dramatically.

For a wonderful, aged effect (particularly on pine) paint on spakfilla (a plaster-of-paris based filler for walls) allow to dry and then sand off. This operation is very dusty, so wear a mask. The white will remain on the low points and come away on the raised areas. If you wish to protect this finish make sure you use a water-based varnish only, as oil-based varnish will discolour the spakfilla unacceptably. The wood can always be varnished first and then the spakfilla applied. Later the spakfilla will gradually wear slightly, which is most attractive.

1. The pig has been sanded, sealed with shellac, re-sanded and then painted with a runny coat of spakfilla. The piece is then left to dry thoroughly.

2. When the spakfilla is absolutely dry, start to sand with 220 sandpaper. This is a very dusty business, so wear a mask to avoid inhaling the dust.

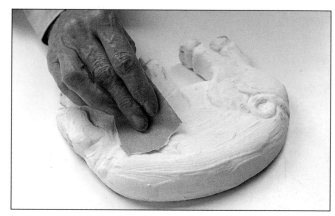

3. The pig, now sanded back so that the spakfilla remains in the lower points only. Do not finish with an oil-based or water-based varnish, as these will discolour the white. If you wish to protect the piece, varnish first, and then apply the spakfilla. Any more wear will prove most desirable.

149

14 |

COLOUR RECIPES

Paint quantities for creating each colour are measured using turpentine-resistant medicine glasses.

THIS CHAPTER IS INTENDED as a guide to mixing your colours for painted finishes. It is necessary to study the examples given for each basic colour and then try to match them with the paints available to you, remembering that different mediums will require varied drying times. When mixing a colour, always combine a tiny amount first and allow to dry before going ahead to mix in the desired quantity. In most cases the colour of the medium you are using will change quite dramatically once it is dry, so it is essential to mix and dry a sample first to prevent later disappointment. Remember that dark colours dry darker and light colours dry slightly lighter.

Painted finishes require very little paint when an antiquing glaze is to be applied. Generally, 30mls of colour mixed with the same amount of scumbling medium will cover an average sized tray. A room measuring 3 x 3 metres will require one litre of colour. Play safe however, and always mix a little more than is required. Keep the leftover covered with cling wrap in case you need to patch at some time. The following recipes should form the basis of a complete mixing repertoire. With this guide you ought to be able to mix almost any colour you desire.

BASE COLOURS

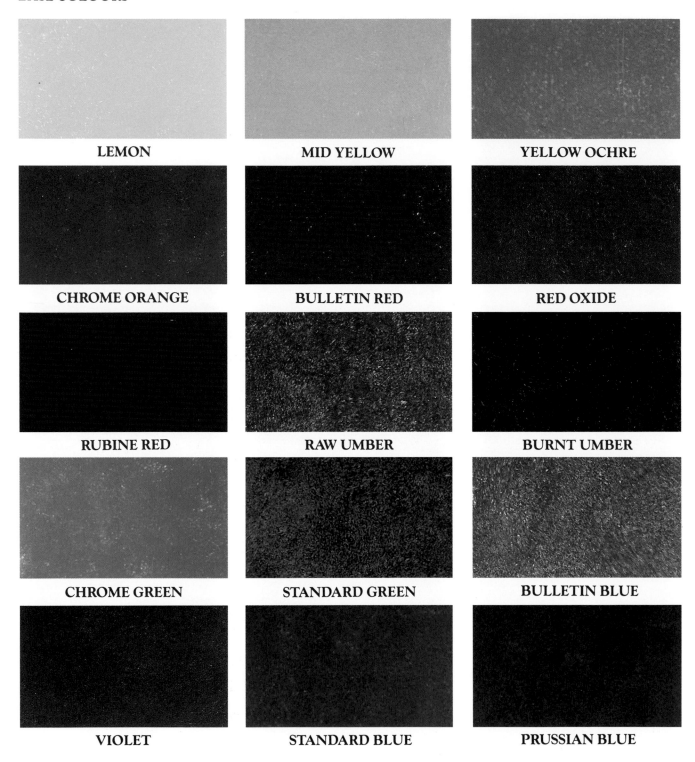

LEMON	MID YELLOW	YELLOW OCHRE
CHROME ORANGE	BULLETIN RED	RED OXIDE
RUBINE RED	RAW UMBER	BURNT UMBER
CHROME GREEN	STANDARD GREEN	BULLETIN BLUE
VIOLET	STANDARD BLUE	PRUSSIAN BLUE

COLOUR RECIPE SWATCHES

Bole for Copper Leaf
30 mls   Burnt Umber
15 mls   Standard Green
2.5 mls Chrome Orange

15 mls   Chrome Green
15 mls   White
2.5 mls Standard Blue

15 mls   Lemon
15 mls   Black
5 mls   Burnt Umber
30 mls   White

15 mls   Chrome Green
15 mls   Lemon
5 mls   Standard Green
2.5 mls Chrome Orange

15 mls   Rubine Red
20 mls   Burnt Umber
15 mls   Chrome Orange
1-2 mls Yellow Ochre

30 mls   White
10 mls   Chrome Orange
10 mls   Yellow Ochre
4-5 mls Raw Umber

Bole for Gold Leaf and Dutch Metal
30 mls   Bulletin Red
15 mls   Chrome Orange
5 mls   Yellow Ochre
3-5 mls Raw Umber

Bole for Silver Leaf
30 mls   White
5 mls   Standard Blue
2.5 mls Chrome Orange
2.5 mls Burnt Umber

Pewter for Aluminium Leaf
12 mls   Raw Umber
12 mls   Burnt Sienna
20 mls   Black
20 mls   White

30 mls   Rubine Red
20-25 mls White
10 mls   Yellow Ochre

30 mls   White
2.5 mls   Bulletin Red
2.5 mls   Yellow Ochre

60 mls   White
4-5 mls   Standard Blue
3 mls   Burnt Umber
Drop Chrome Orange

30 mls   Prussian Blue
3 mls   Violet
12 mls   White

30 mls   White
10 mls   Standard Blue
4-5 mls   Violet

30 mls   White
2.5 mls   Black
1.5 mls   Yellow Ochre
5-7 mls   Raw Umber

45 mls   White
5 mls   Mid Yellow
1 ml   Yellow Ochre

30 mls   White
20 mls   Lemon
1 ml   Yellow Ochre

45 mls   White
5 mls   Mid Yellow
1 ml   Yellow Ochre
1 ml   Chrome Orange

30 mls   White
30 mls   Violet
10 mls   Yellow Ochre

30 mls   White
10 mls   Bulletin Red
3 mls   Yellow Ochre

30 mls   White
6-7 mls   Standard Green
.5-1 ml   Standard Blue
.5-1 ml   Chrome Orange

30 mls   White
6-7 mls   Standard Blue
4 mls   Standard Green
.5-1 ml   Chrome Orange

15 mls   Prussian Blue
20 mls   White
1.5 mls   Violet

15-20 mls White
5 mls   Rubine Red
2.5 mls   Yellow Ochre

30 mls   White
5 mls   Violet
2.5 mls   Yellow Ochre

30 mls   White
10 mls   Lemon
10 mls   Standard Green
5 mls   Chrome Orange

30 mls   White
6 mls   Burnt Umber
5 mls   Chrome Orange
5 mls   Rubine Red
Drop Yellow Ochre

5 mls   Standard Green
5 mls   Burnt Umber
.5 mls   Chrome Orange
30 mls   White

5 mls   Black
1 ml   Raw Umber
1 ml   Yellow Ochre
30 mls   White

5 mls   Black
2.5 mls Yellow Ochre
60 mls   White

Burnt Sienna
10 mls   Burnt Umber
5 mls   Bulletin Red

Raw Sienna
10 mls   Burnt Umber
5 mls   Mid Yellow
.5 mls (or less)
          Chrome Orange

30 mls   Bulletin Blue
30 mls   Chrome Green
5 mls   Raw Umber

30 mls   Bulletin Blue
30 mls   White
1-2 drops
      Chrome Orange

GLOSSARY

Antiquing: The process of creating the appearance of mellowness, age and use.

Aniline dye: This is a natural dye which has been used for centuries. It was discarded by the dyeing industry because of its fugitive (fading) properties. It imparts a natural aged appearance to painted finishes.

Bob: Used to lay on shellac and gold size instead of a brush, a bob helps to eliminate brush strokes in a finish. The bob is made of washed cotton wrapped around a piece of upholstery wadding and secured by a rubber band.

Carnauba wax: Carnauba comes from the leaf of a palm tree grown in Brazil and is a superb wax.

Caustic soda: A powdered substance used with water to remove paint, varnish or shellac.

Chamois: Tanned leather used in painted finishes.

Distress: To age, giving a painted piece the appearance of mellowness and use.

Dragging: The activity of pulling a brush through a glaze to create a series of fine lines.

Drift: Marble always has drifts of stone running through it. A marble finish, in order to be realistic, must have the same drifts.

Ferrule: The metal section of a brush which holds the hairs together.

Fixative: Glue.

Floating: The activity of using a medium (kerosene or turpentine) on which to impose a glaze. The medium disperses the glaze and causes reticulation of the paint.

French polish: This is a purified version of shellac.

Fugitive: Disappearing or fading of colour.

Gild: To impose gold, silver, Dutch metal, copper or aluminium leaf on a surface which has been sized with a mordant.

Glaze: A semi-transparent coat of paint super- imposed over a paler colour, thus creating an appearance of depth. The word does not refer to gloss, simply to a series of colours laid over paler colours.

Glaze coat: *See* Scumble medium.

Isolate: To impose a layer of shellac over a prepared background so that it is impervious to any finish laid over it.

Japan paint: In the 18th century the British tried to emulate Chinese and Japanese lacquer finishes. The activity was called 'japanning' and the paints used were coachpainters' paints. Essentially flat, oil- based enamel paints and dark in colour, these paints are used for the finishes in this book.

Laying off: The activity of the final sweep of a brush over paint after it has been painted on. This term is used by commercial painters.

Mordant: Glue.

Negative antiquing glaze: A negative glaze is laid on with a brush and partially removed with a tool.

Overglaze: A mixture of paint and mineral turpentine imposed over a finish to add depth.

Oxidant: A chemical which oxidises gilding leaf to create an aged appearance.

Positive antiquing glaze: A positive glaze laid on with a brush or tool.

Pounce: To stipple.

Puddle: To drop puddle-like amounts of oxidant onto a piece.

Rottenstone: Very finely ground powder often seen as a grey dust on gilded frames. Used as an ageing medium in painted finishes, and as a burnisher by French polishers. A member of the pumice family.

Scumble: To lay on an amphorous, drift-like cloud of colour, creating direction in a marble finish.

Scumbling medium: A whiting, linseed oil and mineral turpentine mixture which is combined with oil-based paint to stop sagging, hold the imprint of a tool and extend drying time.

Set up: This is the short amount of time that a glaze takes from when it is applied until it ceases to be workable. It is also the term used when size is ready to accept leaf.

Shellac: Insects called *coccus laccae* that swarm on trees in India, Thailand and Burma cocoon their young in their excreta for protection. Twigs, leaves and insects are collected, boiled, strained and purified, eventually to become shellac which is orange. Bleached white shellac is used as an isolating medium in finishes, often called French polish.

Size: Varnish-based glue solution with additives to slow down and keep the drying time even when gilding. "Sizing" refers to the activity of applying size to a surface which is to be gilded.

Skewings: Small pieces of either gold, silver, Dutch metal, copper or aluminium leaf which are created during the process of gilding. They can be saved and used for another finish or used to patch skips on a gilded surface.

Skips: Unsized areas in gilding.

Spatter: To impose paint in tiny dots using a specially cut brush.

Stained edges: Edges of a paint glaze which have a stronger colour than the centre of the glaze.

Stippling: The activity of using a special brush to impress tiny hair-like marks in a glaze to add depth.

Stripping: The activity of removing the paint, shellac or varnish from a piece using special stripper.

Tachiste: The term used for a water-based paint used over silver or aluminium leaf.

Tamp: To run a brush over a gilded surface to ensure adherence of leaf and to remove skewings.

Tuffbacking: An old term used in Europe and the USA to describe wet-sanding.

Wet-sanding: The activity of sanding with water to achieve a silken finish using wet and dry sandpaper.

METRIC CONVERSION TABLE

QUANTITY	METRIC UNIT	IMPERIAL UNIT	METRIC TO IMPERIAL UNITS	IMPERIAL TO METRIC UNITS
LENGTH	millimetre (mm) 10 mm = 1 cm centimetre (cm) 100 cm = 1 m metre (m)	inch (in) foot (ft) yard (yd)	1 cm = 0.394 in 1 m = 3.28 ft 1 m = 1.09 yd	1 in = 25.4 mm 1 ft = 30.5 cm 1 yd = 0.914 m
MASS	gram (g) 1000 g = 1 kg kilogram (kg)	ounce (oz) pound (lb)	1 g = 0.0353 oz 1 kg = 2.20 lb	1 oz = 28.3 g 1 lb = 454 g
VOLUME (fluids)	millilitre (mL) 1000 mL = 1L litre (L)	fluid ounce (fl oz) pint (pt) gallon (gal)	1 mL = 0.0352 fl oz 1 L = 1.76 pint	1 fl oz = 28.4 mL 1 pint = 568 mL 1 gal = 4.55 L
TEMPERATURE	Celsius temp (°C)	Fahrenheit temp (°F)	°F = $\frac{9}{5}$ x °C +32	°C = $\frac{5}{9}$ x (°F-32)

REFERENCE LIST

The following books may prove useful by providing further inspiration or technical information about paint finishes.

Bishop, A. and Lord, C. *The Art of Decorative Stencilling* (Viking Press, New York, and Thames & Hudson, London, 1976)

Desaint, A. *Decoration de Bois et Marbles* Editions H. Vial, (Eyrolles, 1982)

Fales, D.A., Jr. *American Painted Furniture 1660-1880* (E.P. Dutton, New York, 1979)

Hughes, R. and Rowe, M. *The Colouring, Bronzing and Patination of Metals* (The Crafts Council, London, 1982)

Innes, J. *Paint Magic* (Windward, Leicester, England, 1981)

Lipman, J. *American Folk Decoration*, reissued as *Techniques in American Folk Decoration* (Dover Publications, New York, and Constable, London, 1972)

Lipman, J. and Winchester, A. *The Flowering of American Folk Art* (Viking Press, New York, 1974, and Penguin, Harmondsworth, 1977)

Marble Industry Board, *Marble: Vol 1* 41 East 42nd Street, New York, N.Y. 10017

Meyer, F. *Handbook of Ornament* (Dover Publications, New York, 1957)

Milman, M. *Trompe L'Oeil Painting* (Rizzoli, New York, 1983)

O'Neil, I. *The Art of the Painted Finish* (Morrow, New York, 1971)

Pearce, W.J. revised by Hurst, A.E. *Painting and Decorating* (Charles Griffin, London, 8th edition, 1963)

Rhodes, B. and Windsor, J. *Parry's Graining and Marbling* (Collins, London, 1985)

Sayer, R. *The Ladies Amusement* (Ceramic Book Co., Newport, England, 1959)

Sloan, A. and Gwyn, K. *The Complete Book of Decorative Paint Techniques* (Century, London, 1988)

Stalker, J. and Parker, G. *A Treatise of Japanning and Varnishing* (London 1688; new edition, Academy Editions, London, 1971; new edition in 3 vols, Transatlantic Arts, Levittown, 1968)

Stockton, J. *Designer's Guide to Color* (Angus & Robertson, Sydney, 1985)

Waring, J. *Early American Stencils on Walls and Furniture* (Dover Publications, New York and Constable, London, 1968)

U.S. SUPPLIERS

Cabin Craft Southwest
P.O. Box 876
Bedford, TX 76095
(800) 877-1515
(817) 571-3837

Capri Arts & Crafts
P.O. Box 24696, Department D
San Jose, CA 95154
(800) 826-7777

Chatham Art Distributors Inc.
11 Brookside Avenue
Chatham, NY 12037
(800) 822-4747
(518) 392-6300

Chroma Acrylics
(800) 257-8278
(609) 261-8500

Cupboard Distributing
P.O. Box 148DA
Urbana, OH 43078

Dalverwood Art Products
6820 Orangethorpe Avenue, Suite G
Buena Park, CA 90620
(800) 654-2581

DonJer Products Corp.
Ilene Court, Bldg. 8H
Bellemead, NJ 08502

Hofcraft
P.O. Box 1791 Department DAW
Grand Rapids, MI 49501
(800) 828-0359

Ivy Crafts Imports
5410 Annapolis Road
Bladensburg, MD 20710
(301) 779-7079

Kerry Specialties
P.O. Box 5129
Deltona, FL 32728-5129
(407) 574-6209

Koh-I-Noor Inc.
100 North Street
Bloomsbury, NJ 08804
(908) 479-4124

The Painting Peasants
2145 Slater Street
Santa Rosa, CA 95404
(707) 526-1730

Shirley Wilson's LadyBug Art Center
1901 East Bennett
Springfield, MO 65804
(417) 883-4708

SourceLetter
Department DA3A
7509 Seventh Place SW
Seattle, WA 98106

Stan Brown's Arts & Crafts, Inc.
13435 N.E. Whitaker Way
Portland, OR 97230
(800) 547-5531
(503) 257-0559

CANADIAN SUPPLIERS

Folk Art Enterprises Inc.
37 Main Street East
Box 1088
Ridgetown, Ontario
Canada N0P 2C0
(800) 265-9434
(519) 674-0101

Green Lane Folk Art Studio
93 Green Lane
Thornhill, Ontario
Canada L3T 6K6
(416) 882-6346

Heritage Craft Folk Art Studio Inc.
520 Westney Road. S.
Suite 23
Ajax, Ontario
Canada L1S 6W6
(800) 263-3161
(416) 427-6666

Koh-I-Noor Inc.
1815 Meyerside Drive
Mississauga, Ontario
Canada L5T 1G3
(416) 670-0300

Stonehouse Folk Art
RR #2
Oakwood, Ontario
Canada K0M 2M0
(705) 357-3204